By Small and Simple Things

Anita R. Canfield

BOOKCRAFT
Salt Lake City, Utah

Library of Congress Catalog Card Number 99-71853
ISBN 1-57008-654-0

First Printing, 1999

Printed in the United States of America

"But behold I say unto you,
that by small and simple things are
great things brought to pass."
—Alma 37:6

Contents

One	A Path of Duty	1
Two	To Act and Not Be Acted Upon	19
Three	"And On, On to the Victory"	45
Four	For Such a Time As This	73
Five	Learn of Him	95
	Index	118

CHAPTER ONE

A Path of Duty

What is true greatness?

We are constantly being indoctrinated regarding the world's definition of greatness. Our exposure to the limitless talents of renowned musicians, artists, builders, and entrepreneurs is at times overwhelming. Constantly in advertising campaigns we see perfect faces, perfect bodies, beautiful clothing, highly engineered cars, and many luxuries and passions that successful people partake of.

Although I can see that exposure to some of these things can be good for us, because it can serve as motivation to improve our lives, I also see that we often allow ourselves to feel unfulfilled, inadequate, or unsuccessful. I am thinking about those who dwell on their failures while ignoring the elements of their lives that contain true greatness.

What is true greatness?

Most of us are going to miss out on what are supposedly life's biggest prizes—an Oscar, an Emmy, a Tony, a Pulitzer, or even a Nobel. A handful of us may achieve fame across the world. A few more may be known from coast to coast, and perhaps many more will be well known in their own communities.

But most of us, the majority of us, will come to earth and

then leave, having been intimately associated with less than a hundred people.

How can we, then, as individuals, really, truly—not just philosophically, but *really*—know true greatness?

What is true greatness?

Achieving true greatness is a long-term process. There is no such thing as instant greatness. It is never the result of chance or luck and it doesn't come because of a one-time victory. However, it *is* within the reach of all those who are in the gospel net.

True greatness—becoming great men and women—involves doing our best in the day-to-day living of life, especially among the sudden stops and abrupt jolts of struggles, both ordinary and extraordinary.

In 1905 President Joseph F. Smith said, "After all, to do well those things which God ordained to be the common lot of mankind, is truest greatness" (*Juvenile Instructor*, 15 Dec. 1905, p. 752).

The "common lot" of mankind is our work, our ordinary work in temporal and spiritual matters. It is the trials that come equally and commonly to each of us. It is our living and dying in a world that is telestial. To "do well" this work is to strive for "a far better land of promise" (Alma 37:45) and to trust in the Lord enough to have great joy in that striving.

To do well the common lot of mankind, then, is true greatness.

True greatness is the small, quiet, yet significant acts of service and love rendered to our spouses, our children, our extended family, and our friends, neighbors, and coworkers.

True greatness is our time, talent, and resources given unbegrudgingly to build chapels, temples, programs, and, most important, to feed, clothe, and succor the weakest around us. It is giving time, talents, and resources with faith—even enough faith to be great home teachers and visiting teachers, and to be not only servants to the Lord but also shepherds of his flock. It is through the dedication of our own resources that we become great by building others physically, spiritually, and socially.

True greatness is loyalty—to our husbands and wives, to our children and parents, to our brothers and sisters and other loved ones. It is loyalty to our country, our employer, our community. It is to be true and faithful to the Redeemer, loyal to his commandments and to our testimonies. It is to be loyal to our path of duty.

True greatness is to have enough faith and commitment to submit to the Father's will, to endure afflictions, disappointments, tragedies, and chastening with humility and patience. It is to trust, really trust, in the Lord and allow him to work with us, to school us in all things that we need in order to become great men and great women.

And last but not least, true greatness is to desire, to really try, to be of one heart and one mind with Jesus Christ so that, in the end, the effect of our lives on the lives of others can assure us that "when he shall appear we shall be like him" (Moroni 7:48). Today, right now, we should try to grasp why the Lord values the common lot ordinary work of life so highly. We should try to understand here and now that this ordinary work will give us much more than rising with him at the last day, much, much more than living with him for all eternity. This common lot work will make us more and more like him. True greatness is to become like Jesus Christ. I cannot think of anyone or anything greater that I want to be.

I believe that if you will look inside yourself sincerely, you who are reading these words will feel the same way and have those same yearnings of the heart.

What can truly help us to reach such an incredible level of greatness? How can we really become of one heart and one mind with the Savior so that we can become more and more like him?

I believe we hear the answer to those questions every single Sunday in the simple sacramental instruction and commitment to "always remember him" (D&C 20:77). If ever there was a need, these are the days for remembering him.

True greatness is to always remember him and keep the commandments he has given us. This "common lot" work of keeping covenants and commandments may seem unspectacular. There may be those who would question how this ordinary doctrine could be associated with such a supernal concept as becoming great men and women. But Elder Neal A. Maxwell has written: "What seems so plain—keeping the commandments in one's daily life—is 'it!' There is not something else of a higher order which we are supposed to be doing instead.

"This spiritual reality may seem unspectacular, even ordinary, especially if one assumes that some more important and more glamorous chore awaits beyond the horizon. To keep the commandments and to honor our covenants—whether one is a cashier at a grocery checkout counter, a neurosurgeon, an automotive mechanic, or a government official—is what matters, daily and eternally (see Luke 9:23). Each individual is to give away his sins, to deny himself, to lose himself, and then to find himself and full and everlasting joy" (A *Wonderful Flood of Light* [Salt Lake City: Bookcraft, 1990], p. 103).

President Heber J. Grant said: "There is but one path of safety to the Latter-day Saints, and that is the path of duty. It is not testimony, it is not marvelous manifestations, it is not knowing that the Gospel of Jesus Christ is true, . . . it is not actually knowing that the Savior is the Redeemer, and that Joseph Smith was His prophet, that will save you and me, but it is the keeping of the commandments of God, the living the life of a Latter-day Saint" ("The President Speaks," *Improvement Era*, Nov. 1936, p. 659).

Living the life of a Latter-day Saint is what will not only save us in the end but is actually what will make us great men and women.

My daughter's mother-in-law, Marilyn, shared with Ashley how her testimony had been developed. Marilyn told her of the day that she was sitting in fast-and-testimony meeting when her first child was being blessed. Silently, in her heart, she yearned that day to be able to be one who could stand and bear a powerful witness of spiritual experiences; she wished that she possessed an overwhelming knowledge that the Church was true. But she felt distant from that kind of a testimony. She couldn't say those things because she hadn't experienced them at that time in her life.

My daughter knew that Marilyn had grown up in a home where the gospel had not been a priority. Her parents had been inactive, and she had gone to church on her own. Ashley asked her what it was, in her youth, that had prompted her to attend church and be active; and why it was that, as a young woman, she had married in the temple and remained faithful without what she was calling "a strong testimony."

Marilyn answered simply that deep in her heart she knew it was the best thing for her to do. Somehow she realized that living that kind of a life would make her a better person, a better woman, a better wife and mother. And over the years, even though she didn't begin with it, a powerful and eternal testimony of truthfulness has come from simply living the life of a Latter-day Saint, from following a path of duty.

Living this life and following this path of duty hasn't anything to do with perfect people, but rather with people who want to be perfected. And even then, if that desire grows cold, or we forget to do our duty, or we forget about God, he still helps us to remember him. He does it because he loves us and hears the prayers of our righteous loved ones in our behalf. And he helps us remember him because he wants us to return to him, not because he wants to just punish us. So it was with the family of Lehi: "Therefore, as they were unfaithful they did not prosper nor progress in their journey, but were driven back, and incurred the displeasure of God upon them; and therefore they were smitten with famine and sore afflictions, to stir them up in remembrance of their duty" (Mosiah 1:17).

Living a life of duty is what will save us, said President Grant. The Lord will help us. He gives us commandments to keep, callings to fulfill, work to do, people to care about and care for—in short, he gives us the common lot work of mankind. "Therefore there was a law given them, yea, a law of performances and of ordinances . . . to keep them in remembrance of God and their duty towards him" (Mosiah 13:30). Too frequently we forget that this common lot work is not *our* work; it is the Lord's work. It is part of his well-designed earth life and plan for salvation. When we do his work, we are entitled to his help.

The Lord doesn't require us to understand the commandments perfectly, nor does he expect that we will be perfect in keeping them. Perfect people wouldn't need a Savior. I believe he doesn't even ask that we agree with him. He asks us to obey, to simply do our duty because, as my daughter's mother-in-law said, deep within we know it is a path to something better for us. Something eternal within us, this drive embedded within us is the way to greatness.

If we will obey simply for the sake of obedience, or duty, we will experience a remission of sins: "Fulfilling the commandments bringeth remission of sins; and the remission of sins bringeth meekness; . . . and because of meekness . . . cometh the visitation of the Holy Ghost, which Comforter filleth with hope" (Moroni 8:25–26). This hope includes a feeling that the Church is true, that Jesus is the Christ, that God loves us and is helping to bring us home, and that we are becoming better men and women on our way to greatness.

This is the most incredible doctrine! If we will be humble enough to pay a full tithing, accept a Church calling when it is extended, obey the Word of Wisdom, keep the Sabbath holy, attend our meetings, care for one another, and strive to keep all other commandments, we will be blessed with the spirit of meekness. Obedience, even if it is done simply out of duty, will immediately bless us with a spirit of meekness. When we are meek, the Holy Ghost comes to us. He visits us and teaches and comforts us. We are given the witness and testimony that what we are doing is God's work, and that true principles are involved. When we do his work, we are entitled to his help. If paying tithing is difficult for some, when they pay it out of simple obedience they will be given a spirit of meekness. The Holy Ghost will then come to them and will bring witnesses of this true doctrine into their lives and bestow blessings on their lives.

As we obey, do our duty, live the life of a Latter-day Saint, we will experience a remission of our sins. We will "have no more disposition to do evil, but to do good continually" (Mosiah 5:2). We will become more and more meek. We will experience the visitation of the Holy Ghost more continually and consistently. We will feel his daily influence more profoundly. He will help us do our work, which is the Lord's work. He will help us move towards greatness.

As we "do well" the common lot work of mankind, the Holy Ghost will bring such peace and power into our lives that we will be able to "endure it well" (D&C 121:8).

And the promise of greatness in doing our duty, in doing well our common lot work? "All those that have believed, . . . those that have kept the commandments of God, shall come forth in the first resurrection. . . . They are raised to dwell with God who has redeemed them; thus they have eternal life through Christ" (Mosiah 15:22–23).

Those who come forth in the first resurrection are great men and great women. After living the life of a Latter-day Saint, they will inherit eternal life, the life that God and Jesus live!

"Wherefore, now let every man learn his duty, and to act . . . in all diligence" (D&C 107:99).

And what exactly does it mean to live the life of a Latter-day Saint?

"And now my beloved brethren, I have said these things unto you that I might awaken you to a sense of your duty to God, that ye may walk blameless before him. . . . And now I would that ye should be humble, and be submissive and gentle; easy to be entreated; full of patience and long-suffering; being temperate in all things; being diligent in keeping the commandments of God at all times; asking for whatsoever things ye stand in need, both spiritual and temporal; always returning thanks unto God for whatsoever things ye do receive. And see that ye have faith, hope, and charity, and then ye will always abound in good works. And may the Lord bless you, and keep your garments spotless, that ye may at last be brought to sit down with Abraham, Isaac, and Jacob, and the holy prophets who have been ever since the world began, having your garments spotless even as their garments are spotless, in the kingdom of heaven to go no more out" (Alma 7:22–25).

Those who "go no more out" will be the great men and great women who have walked a path of duty.

Elder Henry B. Eyring has written of his father, whose name was also Henry Eyring. The older Eyring was an accomplished scholar and scientist. More than that, he was a member of the Church who believed as President Grant did that we have a "path of duty."

When he was almost eighty years old, Brother Eyring had bone cancer in his hips to the degree that he could hardly move and was in excruciating pain.

At this time of his life his high council duties included responsibility for the stake welfare farm. The stake had been given an assignment to weed a field of onions, so Brother Eyring assigned himself to go work on the farm.

Several people who were there that day later told his son how hard it had been for this humble man. They said that his pain had been so great that they watched him all day pulling himself along his stomach with his elbows. The pain was so intense that he could not even kneel. But these same people also reported that his father had smiled and laughed and was full of life and happiness as they worked together in the onion fields.

In Elder Eyring's own words: "After all the work was finished and the onions were all weeded, someone said to him, 'Henry, good heavens! You didn't pull those weeds, did you? Those weeds were sprayed two days ago, and they were going to die anyway.'

"Dad just roared. He thought that was the funniest thing. He thought it was a great joke on himself. He had worked through the day in the wrong weeds. They had been sprayed and would have died anyway.

"When Dad told me this story, I knew how tough it was. So I asked him, 'Dad, how could you make a joke out of that? How could you take it so pleasantly?' He said something to me that I will never forget, and I hope you won't. He said, 'Hal, I wasn't there for the weeds.'

"Now you'll be in an onion patch much of your life. So will I. It will be hard to see the powers of heaven magnifying us or our efforts. It may even be hard to see our work being of any value at all. And sometimes our work won't go well.

"But you didn't come for the weeds. You came for the Savior.

9

And if you pray, and if you choose to be clean, and if you choose to follow God's servants, you will be able to work and wait long enough to bring down the powers of heaven.

"I was with my Dad in the White House in Washington, D.C., the morning he got the National Medal of Science from the president of the United States. I missed the days when he got all the other medals and prizes. But, oh, how I'd like to be with him on the morning he gets the prize he won for his days in the onion patches. He was there to wait on the Lord. And you and I can do that, too." (Henry B. Eyring, *To Draw Closer to God* [Salt Lake City: Deseret Book Co., 1997], pp. 101–2).

The gospel of Jesus Christ is God's pattern for happiness and joy here in this life and in the world to come. It makes possible the lofty goal of greatness, of becoming like the Savior. Satan is hard at work trying to deceive us into believing that there are other paths that will be all right to travel. But if we are to achieve daily spiritual safety and then eternal happiness, we need to walk the one and only true road home. That road is through the commandments of God.

Brigham Young made this statement: "There is not a man of us but what is willing to acknowledge at once that God demands strict obedience to his requirements. But in rendering that strict obedience, are we made slaves? No, it is the only way on the face of the earth for you and me to become free, and we shall become slaves of our own passions, and of the wicked one, and servants to the devil, if we take any other course" (in *Journal of Discourses* 18:246).

Recently I heard someone comment that the world today is as wicked as the days of Noah. If we calculate Noah's family versus the entire population at that time, maybe mathematically the proportion of righteous people versus the unrighteous would be the same today. Only eight people were spared then—eight *righteous* people. Today there are millions, and many millions more coming. I have great hope in the Saints of this world, for even though it is filled with wickedness, many "of them are in the path of their duty, and they do walk circumspectly before God, and they do observe to keep the commandments and his statutes" (Helaman 15:5).

As we go to our jobs and our careers, buy groceries, pay bills, do laundry, prepare lessons, attend church, have family home evening, render service to others, attend the temple, teach our children to pray, help them with their homework, and then, before we retire at night, deal with a crisis from time to time, do we ever get a sense of the greatness that is in the making?

I met an elderly couple in central Canada who seemed to have lived ordinary lives, yet in their presence I felt an uncommon spirit.

They had sustained themselves temporally through their adult lives by farming. They had owned a modest but comfortable home near the town, and their farm property had been in a more rural area outside the town. During the years they were rearing their children they lived lives common to Latter-day Saints. They were active in church, they attended the temple, and they sent many of their children on missions. All of their children had married in the temple.

They were nearing retirement when the economy in their province went sour. The economic crisis threw many businesses and services into turmoil and financial straits. As a result, they lost their farm and their life savings. However, with the assistance of some of their children they managed to scrape together the funds to save their home and belongings. They were too old now to ever recover financially, and there would only be enough money through pensions to meagerly cover living expenses for the remainder of their lives.

And then, about one year later, they were called on to continue in a path of duty. A call to serve a full-time mission in a foreign land was issued to them. In order for them to be able to go they would have to sell their home and most of their possessions. But this little couple had not come to this life for the possessions or goods of the earth, but for the treasures of heaven and the greatness in themselves. They sold all that they had and served for eighteen months in a foreign land.

When I met them, their dreams of living out their last years in their comfortable, safe little home were gone forever. They now lived in a modest apartment building and rented, not owned, a one-bedroom flat. Their possessions now amounted to mismatched, somewhat shabby but clean thrift store purchases. Some ward members had contributed a table here, a chair or two there. It was very, very humble.

But not as humble as I felt when they invited me in and I crossed that threshold. I was immediately overcome with such a power of love and was so enveloped by a spirit of peace that I was hard-pressed to restrain my tears. I could not take my eyes off of their faces. They radiated, almost glowed. Their demeanor was so amazingly gentle and so incredibly powerful at the same time. I felt loved. I felt I was in the presence of angels. I felt like this abode was a place of refuge, a temple. I had not expected to feel these things, these emotions. But I left there several hours later filled with a desire *to be like them.*

I have no idea whether in their youth they were handsome or smart or clever. I know nothing of their education or if their former home was remarkable. I don't know if they had any special talents or could even sing a note. Certainly farming isn't a glamorous career, and they probably never had a fancy car.

But I left wanting to be like them. I felt their greatness and felt that they were "worthy of a far more, and an exceeding, and an eternal weight of glory" (D&C 132:16).

When I flew in to the Salt Lake airport one time on my way to Education Week at Brigham Young University I witnessed the results of those who are "anxiously engaged" along a path of duty. It was Tuesday morning, and Tuesdays are the usual day when missionaries leave the Missionary Training Center in Provo for their various missions around the world. There, crowded at almost every gate of every airline, were the young men and young women wearing those familiar name tags—young adults who were ready and willing to "deny themselves" and give up part of their youthful time on earth to labor among the people of the world.

But the ones I watched that Tuesday morning were the mothers. They had come to see their children off. They had come to grasp one last hug, one last kiss, one last glimpse of this youthful life they had sheltered, protected, encouraged, and prepared for so many years.

The next day, on Wednesday, as I drove by the Missionary Training Center I saw the common Wednesday routine underway. Wednesday is the day for new arrivals to enter the Missionary Training Center. Here I saw another set of mothers, hugging and clutching those sons and daughters, hanging on to every precious moment.

Mothers in Zion walk the path of duty to prepare their sons and daughters in order to give them back to the Lord. I know what they were feeling, those women at the airport and the Missionary Training Center—I have taken three of my children there. It takes about twenty years of ordinary, unglamorous work for a mother to get her child there. And then that mother is unable to see or touch or share immediately in that child's life for two years. After a lifetime of working so hard to make holidays and birthdays traditional and meaningful family experiences, I know a little of the loss a mother feels when she sees the empty chair.

But every Tuesday at the Salt Lake City airport and every Wednesday at the Missionary Training Center, mothers bring their sons and daughters to send them forth on a path of duty, to do the common lot work of mankind.

And frequently, waiting for them in the mission field are other members who also are traveling a path of duty: members who at times will feed those Elders and Sisters, even when they have nothing much to eat themselves; members who live in shacks and shanties and dress in rags; members who are so poor that they go hungry the day after they feed the missionaries. And there are also members waiting in the many wards around the world who help the missionaries in their service by giving referrals and having investigators taught in their homes.

Thus, the path of duty of one mother can reach across continents and eventually generations to touch the lives of many, many of God's other children.

An accountant in my stake became interested in the life of an early pioneer woman who crossed the plains after the exodus from Nauvoo. Her story is filled with devastating hardship, severe trials, and tragedies of every kind. Her suffering was not always physical. On one occasion the Lord required her to give up her very young son to the Mormon Battalion. She bore a heavy load, as did so many of those particularly great men and great women.

This brother in my stake wondered if her ordinary life— which had been made so exceedingly more difficult because of the dire circumstances of those early Saints—had really made a difference.

Through her faith and perseverance, she led her family across the plains to a "far better land of promise." Her legacy of testimony reaches today down through the generations. This accountant calculated, first on the basis of her five children who survived, how large would be her posterity today. The number exceeded thirty thousand. But that's not all. Two of her sons filled full-time missions. He computed that if every twenty years, two of her posterity had served missions, the number of individuals who would have heard the gospel message or may have been touched indirectly or directly by her posterity would have exceeded ten million people!

On the mud-packed trail, in the drizzling rain, under the searing hot desert sun, surrounded by hungry children, unable to do much else except survive—I wonder if this great woman understood that through her path of duty she had "come to the kingdom for such a time as this" (Esther 4:14; see verses 10–16). I wonder if she knew that through her common lot work she would bless the lives of so many.

Elder David B. Haight said: "Brothers and sisters, live the commandments. Do what is right. Take advantage of this great opportunity in your life to live it well, to be good, to have good works, and to influence other people for good. The gospel is true. I hope that every day of my life I might be able to do some good and to encourage somebody to live a better life and to understand what has been restored to the earth" ("Live the Commandments," *Ensign*, May 1998, p. 8).

One of my sons had planned all of his life to go on a mission. When he turned eighteen and a half his plans changed. In fact, he grew further and further away from not only a mission but also his spirituality.

As his nineteenth birthday approached, his dad and I tried to open a discussion with him about his mission. He didn't want to talk about it. So we took him on a three-day camping trip, though personally I would rather slam my hand in a car door than go camping! Because he knew this about his mother, he realized how much we wanted to understand his heart and his thoughts. During that trip he expressed some concerns over his future, concerns over the unknowns, concerns that his testimony was truly his own. The talks drew us all closer, but he still did not want to go on a mission.

He turned nineteen on a Sunday. That Saturday evening before his birthday I went into his room to say good night and tried one more time to say words that would inspire him to reconsider.

Instead, he became more upset with me and told me he felt that I was trying too hard to persuade him to go. He let me know he felt I was wrong to discuss this with him and that my thoughts were no longer welcome. He said, "I don't think I *want* to go. I think if you go on a mission you ought to have the *desire* to go. It has to be your desire and you have to think it will be good for you to go."

I left his room feeling that I had made the situation worse, really sorry I had said anything more. As I prayed later, I asked for inspiration. What could I do? What should I do? Was there something that would reach him? Should I do nothing more?

As I woke up the next morning a clear and distinct thought came immediately into my mind. I searched through some Church videotapes until I found the message that had come into my mind. I went in his room and woke him up to say happy birthday; then I invited him downstairs in front of the television.

I put in the VCR a video entitled *Family Home Evening,* and told him I was only going to play the first one minute and then turn it off.

The introductory music stopped, and there stood President Ezra Taft Benson addressing the congregation assembled in the Tabernacle in Salt Lake City. In that brief segment he declared that it was the duty of every young man to serve a full-time mission. I turned the tape off as promised, turned to my son, and told him that it would be wonderful if he had the desire to go; that it would be even better if he really wanted to go; but that neither of those things mattered. As spoken from the mouth of a prophet, it was his *duty* to go. And then I promised him that if he would just go out of duty, the desire would come and he would be blessed beyond anything he could ever do on his own. He would become the man he was meant to be.

He didn't seem very happy all day. He was unusually quiet. But that evening, that Sunday evening on his nineteenth birthday, dressed in a shirt and tie, with scriptures in hand, he came downstairs to tell us he was on his way to see the bishop. During the next months of preparation the Holy Ghost came to help my son. He gave him a witness that the preparation was God's work and that true principles were involved. He helped him fill his heart with a sincere and enthusiastic desire to go. A few months later, on a Wednesday afternoon, we took him to the Missionary Training Center in Provo, Utah, to commence his path of duty.

You can imagine the joy we felt over the months that followed as we read of his tremendous love for his mission and for the people, especially for the people. He wrote of his sacrifices and how it was a blessing to him to have this mission and those sacrifices. He wrote of the sorrow at seeing those whom he served reject the gospel and of his utter joy at seeing others accept it. He wrote profound words of his love of the Savior and his deepened testimony of the Prophet Joseph Smith and the Book of Mormon. He wrote very emotionally of his gratitude for being raised in the gospel and knowing the truth. He was called to serve as district leader, then zone leader, and finally assistant to the mission president. He grew in leadership talent, spirituality, faith, and wisdom.

And now that it is time for him to leave his missionary service he has mixed emotions about coming home. I think back on the words of President Benson, and I know there is safety in simply living the life of a Latter-day Saint and doing one's duty to the Lord.

Whether one is a world-famous scientist awarded a medal from the president of the United States, or a brand new mother watching her first child blessed, or an elderly couple being called to serve a mission, or a poverty-stricken citizen living in an obscure village in a third-world country, the path of duty is going to require sacrifices. But through those sacrifices, in similitude of the One and Great Sacrifice, we can become greater men and women.

"Whosoever has heard the words of the prophets, . . . all those who have hearkened unto their words . . . are the heirs of the kingdom of God" (Mosiah 15:11). These are they who did well the common lot of mankind. These are great men and great women.

CHAPTER TWO

To Act and Not Be Acted Upon

It all began in a place I can't remember, this quest for greatness. In fact, it began in a place that none of us can remember. We have been taught truthfully about this premortal realm, and even though we can't recall the vision of it there is something eternal inside our hearts that makes us believe we were in that great, sacred, lovely home where God and his nobles live. There we were instructed, commanded, and then probably told these words, "Thou mayest choose for thyself" (Moses 3:17).

A third part of all in that great family did not choose greatness. Most, if not all, who join The Church of Jesus Christ of Latter-day Saints did.

Later in a garden—a sacred, lovely, and protected place created for two of God's most noble children—the quest for greatness continued. And it continued with those same words, "Thou mayest choose for thyself."

Much later still, another faithful and noble one taught his sons that God created "things to act and things to be acted upon." And he made it very clear that the Lord "gave unto man that he should act for himself" and "not to be acted upon" (2 Nephi 2:14, 16, 26). He taught his sons that they were free to choose and that if they chose to follow the Savior they would find happiness and greatness. But if they chose to follow Satan, they would never find greatness and they would never be happy, because Satan "seeketh that all men might be miserable like unto himself" (2 Nephi 2:27).

Misery! What a great word to describe how we feel when our behavior (or attitude) doesn't match our desire to be great and noble. Miserable is how we feel when we make choices that distance us from greatness.

Godliness and greatness come only through the wise use of our agency. Whether we are miserable or we enjoy this life is largely a consequence of individual choice. The ultimate enjoyment of this life results from accepting, through obedience, God's commandments and from doing all we can to serve him, ever under circumstances that we cannot control.

In other words, we are free to choose but we are expected to choose correctly. Choosing correctly brings peace. If we choose incorrectly, we experience misery. We are then no longer free but become heavy burdened with fear, guilt, anger, self-doubt, and other maladies of poor choices.

But there are many, many who are confused and believe that because they do not feel good about themselves they must be unable to fulfill their potential. They believe they have to struggle through choices and decisions, constantly trying to overcome the handicap of low self-esteem. In fact, many falsely believe their poor or incorrect choices are the result of either low self-esteem or circumstances beyond their control.

The most important message we need to teach one another about potential is that no matter how we feel about ourselves we have the responsibility to make good and correct choices. As God's children, we are among his creations that are "not to be acted upon." Through making good and wise choices we will feel better about ourselves, we will feel our greatness and worth, and we will be happy, truly happy.

I am convinced that our quest for greatness began with the words "Thou mayest choose for thyself," and those choices build a structure on the foundation of obedience.

I am well acquainted with foundations and structures. In my thirty-year career as an architectural interior designer I have observed that large, magnificent structures require substantial foundations with massive footings. One project, a forty-five story hotel, had a foundation that resembled an underground cement city.

A foundation of sustained, substantial obedience allows us year after year to add on the virtues and qualities of greatness. The structure built on a foundation of obedience will bring us closer to greatness, closer to the Savior, so that "when he shall appear we shall be like him" (Moroni 7:48).

How does it work? Why does it work this way and no other?

"The fulfilling the commandments bringeth remission of sins; and the remission of sins bringeth meekness, and lowliness of heart; and because of meekness and lowliness of heart cometh the visitation of the Holy Ghost, which Comforter filleth with hope and perfect love . . . until the end shall come" (Moroni 8:25–26).

Special power comes to those who are baptized into the Church of Jesus Christ and continue in the faith by choosing to obey the commandments. Obedience immediately brings the gift of meekness, which brings the visitation of the Holy Ghost. The Holy Ghost speaks of "things as they really are, and of things as they really will be" (Jacob 4:13). Through our wise and correct choices he can fill our hearts with an overwhelming witness that we have done the right thing. He can show us and help us feel our worth. We can receive further witnesses of the truths we have been taught. He will inspire us and actually help us feel love—for God, from God, for ourselves, and for each other. And he will fill us with hope, enough hope to choose correctly again, and again, and then again. This love and hope will deepen and widen the foundation upon which we structure our character and emulate the Savior. He will truly be our comforter as we overcome behavior unbecoming a god and replace it by obedience with greatness (see Mosiah 5:2).

Obedience doesn't mean perfection. The Savior isn't waiting for us to be perfectly obedient before he will help us. That's not the unrelenting demand of obedience in this life. The Savior does require "the heart and a willing mind" (D&C 64:34). He also wants us to find out something about ourselves. He wants us to discover that we love him, that we have always loved him, that we want to be like him, that we are willing to do whatever it takes to become as he is. And one more important piece of information—he wants us to realize that we need him, that he wants to help us home, and that he really, truly loves us and has always loved us. This is why obedience is the real key to self-esteem. No matter how we feel about ourselves, no matter what our circumstances, we need to make good, wise, and just choices if we are to empower ourselves to nobility and greatness.

Sister Chieko Okazaki wrote of the willingness to commit our love to the Savior in this way: "God wants you—not somebody else, not you in ten years, not a perfect you, but you right now. Consider this experience of Sharon Lee Swenson, a faculty member at Brigham Young University, when she was called as Relief Society president in her ward in Salt Lake City:

"'All my life, I have felt that someday I would be great and valuable. Someday. Not now, not yet. But someday, I'd do everything just right. I'd be slim, attractive, and soft-spoken, without a semi-lisp and southern Utah drawl. When I opened my dresser drawers, I would see neatly folded clothes with crocheted sachets nestled among them. I would have a spotless refrigerator filled with healthy, delicious food. I'd read poetry and would have abandoned my current need for regular doses of strong murder mysteries. But I knew I wasn't that person then.

"'The witness I received . . . was that the Lord wanted me—murder mysteries, mixed-up drawers, and all, complete with failings and weaknesses. I was loved of the Lord and had something important to give my sisters. That something was I, myself'" ("The Amazement of Grace," *Dialogue*, Winter 1988, p. 98.)

"That's all the Lord wants of you—you, yourself. And that's all you can give. You can't be someone you aren't. You can't give someone else's gift. Who and what you are is enough, and each gift, given like this, is glorious! The Doctrine and Covenants explains, 'The Lord requireth the heart and a willing mind.' (D&C 64:34.) It doesn't say that the Lord requires competence, or a Ph.D., or immaculate housekeeping, or professional success. But it doesn't say that he'll be satisfied with a half-hearted you, either. He wants your whole heart, and for a good reason. Real power does not lie in external forces, but in the heart" (*Lighten Up!* [Salt Lake City: Deseret Book Co., 1993], p. 69).

When we give the Savior our hearts, and when our minds are willing to be obedient, our yearning and commitment to greatness are acceptable to the Lord, even if some of our behavior isn't. He knows that as long as our hearts and minds are fully committed, our inappropriate behavior will continue to disturb us. He then has a life he can work with. He will see to it that we have experiences that will make us think with those willing minds and feel with those tender hearts until change comes. We will, through obedience, be inspired to choose better, deed by deed, word by word, thought by thought, until we discover our greatness.

Our Father in Heaven will not change our hearts or minds against our will. Remember the words "Thou mayest choose for thyself"? Those words were not meant to set us up for failure. He didn't mean, "You are carnal; you are weak, stupid, and disgusting beings. Go ahead, just see if you can do it right!" He gave us commandments so that through obedience we could discover that we really are like him. Change happens because we awaken to that perspective. Our hearts are stirred and we feel in our hearts "no more disposition to do evil, but to do good continually" (Mosiah 5:2).

Doing good continually and losing the disposition to do evil has nothing to do with being perfect and everything to do with accepting a path of duty. As long as we are doing things to consistently remember the Lord, be accountable, and repent, we are being obedient. If we are being consistent in saying our daily prayers, even if not all those prayers are inspired, we are obedient. If we are attending our meetings, accepting Church callings to serve, and supporting our leaders, we are being obedient. Consistency matters if we want greatness.

Whether our choices of right and wrong are issues of integrity or issues with our thinking process, we are accountable and responsible. Our "natural man" tendencies are toward blaming others or circumstances; we also naturally tend toward self-pity. There are other reasons we use to excuse ourselves from accountability, but these two seem to be most common.

I remember how much I beat myself up for the drug addiction of one of my children. I was the Self-Pity Regent. Then, as I began to look around me, I saw women who were *tremendously* better mothers than I could ever be, women whose lives were beyond reproach, women of great faith and ability. Yet I saw some of their children making mistakes even more serious than mine, even heinous sins. And I saw women who struggled, really struggled, with issues that weren't a problem for me, women whose lives were full of their own seriously poor choices and yet whose children were nearly perfect!

The Lord showed me in those days that my thoughts of failure had no place in the kingdom of God and I had better repent. The realization came that my choices of thought needed to be according to the doctrines I found in scripture, especially those directing me to trust in the Lord and have faith. It would be through my faith that power would come to reclaim and retain my loved ones.

Consider the choices of one of the greatest men to ever walk the earth. He was born into a family well acquainted with the low self-esteem that comes from making poor choices.

His own mother, Rachel, was despised by her blood sister, Leah. Leah displayed a jealous and envious nature because she believed her husband, Jacob, loved Rachel, her sister and his second wife, more than her. These kinds of feelings cannot be hidden very well. If Leah was so affected, it's no wonder Jacob loved Rachel more! The strife among the wives magnified as they began to fortify themselves against each other by even giving their maidservants to Jacob to try to multiply their children through them.

As these children grew, they must have been influenced by the bitterness and contention between their mothers. Children often grow up and carry on the poison of a preceding generation. These children exhibited the lack of love and respect for each other, their parents, and at times their neighbors. In that family there were acts of incest, rape, murder, theft, trickery, deceit, greed, adultery, fornication, hatred, jealousy, and pride of every kind. Choices like these ensure that they won't feel good about themselves.

It is no wonder that when Joseph finally was born, his ten older brothers seemed already pretty miserable with themselves and had no vision of their own greatness. They resented his success. They failed to see that obedience was the only thing that stood between them and Joseph, between them and the same greatness they saw in Joseph. They chose to blame him for their misery instead of making a better, wiser choice to repent.

Perhaps Joseph was a little arrogant when he told them about his dreams of ruling over his brothers, perhaps he may have flaunted the special coat his father gave him—but then, perhaps not! It doesn't matter. We have to remember that he was young and his brothers were older—and should have been wiser. But they chose to blame instead of repent and make an effort to be obedient themselves. We can remember this same scenario repeated later, in another part of the world, by two older brothers named Laman and Lemuel.

Joseph's spiritual greatness is remarkable! His brothers conspired to murder him while they held him hostage in a pit. Can you imagine hearing your family members arguing over whether to kill you? Then they pulled him up out of his hole like a captured animal and sold him into slavery. They knew what they were doing. They knew what his future held. The hopelessness and sorrow of slavery was the ultimate degradation. Yet Joseph's greatness through the life of obedience he had led in his father's home could not be masked even as a slave. "And the Lord was with Joseph, and he was a prosperous man; and he was in the house of his master the Egyptian. And his master saw that the Lord was with him, and that the Lord made all that he did to prosper in his hand" (Genesis 39:2–3). Potiphar, his master, made Joseph overseer of his household and trusted him with all he owned. Joseph's obedience and greatness deepened.

Potiphar's wife tried repeatedly and unsuccessfully to seduce the valiant Joseph. The famous story of his fleeing her advances and her presence, which led to her accusations and his imprisonment, only show us further his deepening greatness because of his continued obedience (see verses 7–23). He probably could have justified himself into making poorer choices. Compare his wise decisions to those immoral acts committed by his brothers. With this kind of character, it becomes more and more clear how he could exude confidence and greatness even as a slave. Character like this comes from good choices, from acting and not being acted upon.

Recently I listened to a world-acclaimed, globally renowned Christian evangelist respond to a question about the moral credibility of our nation's highest official. This minister, to whom millions look for guidance, said that he could understand how this particular leader could have succumbed to temptation. He attributed the poor choices to being too handsome and too desirable—and to experiencing too many women throwing themselves at him. He said we couldn't and shouldn't blame him. He made it clear that he believed it was unavoidable as he justified the choices made. I was stunned, especially when he concluded by calling this leader "a great man."

To me, the great man is the one who said: "Behold, my master . . . hath committed all that he hath to my hand; . . . neither hath he kept back any thing from me but thee, because thou art his wife: how then can I do this great wickedness, and sin against God?" (Genesis 39:8–9).

More powerful still is the realization that in trying to obey God, Joseph was thrown into prison, yet he never blamed God or allowed himself to become bitter.

Potiphar could have had him killed. But I think Potiphar knew his wife, and he knew Joseph, and he knew which one was innocent. But he probably couldn't humiliate his wife and had too much pride to demean himself, so Joseph had to leave. Prison was better than death.

Even there, look what Joseph did. His greatness increased and multiplied because of this tremendous act of obedience and desire to obey God. In the prison "the Lord was with Joseph . . . and gave him favour in the sight of the keeper of the prison" (Genesis 39:21). Soon he was over all the prisoners; and years later, because of the good choices and the Lord's blessings, he ruled over all the land of Egypt, second only to Pharaoh.

Do you think Joseph was a happy-go-lucky sort of fellow who just "rolled with the punches"? Do you think he was able to dismiss his pain and just never look back? The record of his true feelings is brief, but the weight of those feelings bears down through the centuries, and we can more than glimpse his pain and sorrow.

After more than twenty years, when he first saw his brothers again Joseph "spake roughly unto them" (Genesis 42:7; see verses 1–8). Maybe he was struggling to overcome the immediate anger at his tremendous loss, especially the years of being deprived of his beloved father. But Joseph was a great man, and soon compassion overcame him: "He turned himself about from them, and wept" (verse 24). When his brothers returned with his little brother Benjamin, who had grown into manhood since he had last seen him, "Joseph made haste; for his bowels did yearn upon his brother: and he sought where to weep; and he entered into his chamber, and wept there" (Genesis 43:30).

Then came the moment when he could no longer hold back the sorrow and the joy: "Then Joseph could not refrain himself before all them that stood by him; and he cried, Cause every man to go out from me. And there stood no man with him, while Joseph made himself known unto his brethren. And he wept aloud: and the Egyptians and the house of Pharaoh heard. And Joseph said unto his brethren, I am Joseph; doth my father yet live? And his brethren could not answer him; for they were troubled at his presence. And Joseph said unto his brethren, Come near to me, I pray you. And they came near. And he said, I am Joseph your brother, whom ye sold into Egypt. . . . And he fell upon his brother Benjamin's neck, and wept; and Benjamin wept upon his neck. Moreover he kissed all his brethren, and wept upon them: and after that his brethren talked with him. . . . And Joseph made ready his chariot, and went up to meet Israel his father, to Goshen, and presented himself unto him; and he fell on his neck, and wept on his neck a good while" (Genesis 45:1–4, 14–15; 46:29).

Joseph, who had risen to the highest official office in Egypt, had done so because of obedience to God. That obedience had rendered him confident, full of self-esteem and love for others, and more and more Christlike. He was even able to forgive those who had so sorely injured him. Joseph continually made good and wise choices based on obedience, even in circumstances he could not control. He learned that he was free to act for himself, even though many personal freedoms had been taken away.

Commenting on Joseph's experiences, Elder Hartman Rector, Jr., said: "The story of Joseph, the son of Jacob, . . . is a vivid representation of the great truth that 'all things work together for good to [those] who' love God. (See Rom. 8:28.) Joseph always seemed to do the right thing; but still, more importantly, he did it for the right reason. . . . Even as an indentured servant, Joseph turned every experience and all circumstances, no matter how trying, into something good.

"This ability to turn everything into something good appears to be a godly characteristic. Our Heavenly Father always seems able to do this. Everything, no matter how dire, becomes a victory to the Lord. Joseph, although a slave and wholly undeserving of this fate, nevertheless remained faithful to the Lord and continued to live the commandments and made something very good of his degrading circumstances. People like this cannot be defeated, because they will not give up. They have the correct, positive attitude, and Dale Carnegie's expression seems to apply: If you feel you have a lemon, you can either complain about how sour it is, or you can make lemonade. It is all up to you" ("Live Above the Law to Be Free," *Ensign*, Jan. 1973, p. 130).

In other words, "Thou mayest choose for thyself."

I met Hans Smith about two years ago when he and his family moved into our ward.

Hans is a charming and delightful twelve-year-old boy. He is confined to a wheelchair without the use of body and limbs because he has had cerebral palsy from birth. The cause of cerebral palsy is unknown, but part of the brain bleeds and causes severe neurological damage. Hans is classified as severely handicapped. The doctors are amazed he can even speak.

I had the opportunity to spend some time with Hans and would like to share some of his words with you. We were talking about the challenges of being in a wheelchair, and Hans said: "It's so hard for me. It's hard because when I see boys my age playing baseball, I must admit I have been emotional about it. Sometimes I just want to get out there and climb fences, and use a bat, and get in trouble sometimes. I can't swing a bat and so I can't break a window. It seems like that would be great fun to break a window!

"But the nice thing about being LDS is you know it won't be forever. This is a temporary test, and I need to get through it. It is building my character."

As I listened to Hans I wondered if he really believed this, or was he just repeating back words of encouragement from others. In a few more minutes I knew what Hans said was indeed his own conviction, born not of philosophy but of his own experience.

He said, "I believe the reason I was sent here like this was because my Heavenly father knew I had the courage to do it. Some people might say, why did Heavenly Father do this to you? Or why did this happen to me? I believe he loves us very much and we have certain problems because he wants us to find out how great we are. In a sense he believes we are stronger than others.

"Heavenly Father won't ever leave you. He will answer you if you just ask him. But you have to ask with faith, that's the key. You won't get an answer if you say sentences that don't mean anything anymore—like 'Thank you for this nice day.' I know one thing, he is a picky Heavenly Father in the way he wants you to talk to him. He wants us to really be sincere and talk about a lot of stuff."

I asked Hans how he learned to pray.

"I have good parents; they taught me to pray. And I've been in those situations that I'm so desperate for him to answer, I've needed answers. If we hurry or say nothing to him, he won't answer us. We have to be sincere and very private with him.

"There was a time when I really wanted to play baseball. I really wanted to be involved. One of the coaches said he would take me. But he didn't realize how handicapped I am. I can't use my hands. The coach didn't know what to do with me. He said I could wear the uniform and sit with the team. He would try to figure something out if he could."

Hans came home sobbing. He didn't want to wear the uniform and sit on the bench. He wanted to play baseball, and he cried to his mother that that was *not playing* baseball!

That night he offered up a touching prayer to a "picky" Heavenly Father. He told Heavenly Father that he knew he was loved by Him and that Heavenly Father would help him find his way. He knew there was something He could do to help him accomplish what other boys liked to do. He said in essence, "Heavenly Father, this is my situation. Where can I go from here? What can I do?" Hans just wanted to be a boy.

The next morning he woke up and told his mother that an

answer had come. He could sing! Hans is now a member of the Boys Chorus of Southern Nevada. He is actively involved. He was in the training choir for eighteen months, and now he is in the senior choir that tours. He told me, "There are people who help me on and off stage, people to hand me the microphone when I do a solo, people to take it back. It's just great. I just feel regular when I'm there!"

Hans has had many painful surgeries. The most painful one was when the bones in his feet were fused together. Pain is measured on a threshold of one to ten. The pain he suffered after the surgery was so intense and severe, his blood pressure skyrocketed so high that the nurses scaled his pain at fifteen.

For hours his mother worked with the nurses trying to relieve him. The medication wasn't working. They tried loosening the casts and elevating him. As his mother mopped the great drops of perspiration, Hans thought of the Savior: "This pain was more overwhelming than I could ever imagine. I thought of Jesus Christ. What did the Savior go through? It must have been more than this."

Hans told the nurses, "I have to pray." And so this humble little boy raised his voice to the God he knew loved him and begged for relief and mercy.

Within a minute or two he was completely pain free, and Hans said, "I was ready to sleep." By the time his uncle arrived at the hospital to administer to him, Hans was fast asleep. He told me that in that desperate hour, he found out what kind of strength he really has.

He said, "When I have to have surgery I get freaked out. Who wouldn't? I can't swallow the medicine. So Heavenly Father helps me. I pray and he sends a calming feeling and more, a lot more. Every step of the way I know he will be with me. And even if I don't make it, he'll send an angel to come and get me, and I won't ever be alone."

His mother told me that the brain damage is so severe that Hans was not supposed to ever be able to speak. But he has a special message to his fellowmen, a message that we must act for ourselves and not be acted upon. And in order for us to hear this great testimony, Hans had to be able to speak.

When he was five years old he and his mother went to a wheelchair store. There was an elderly gentleman, about mid-seventies, whom Hans became acquainted with. He asked the man why he was in his wheelchair. It was due to a condition brought on by aging. He had spent almost all his life normal. He had been a professor at a large university. He asked Hans why he was in the chair. Hans told him he was born with cerebral palsy. Then, with the brightness of a pure spirit this five-year-old taught the jaded, seasoned intellectual the gospel message. He talked about the next life and being resurrected and having a whole body.

The old man approached Hans's mother, amazed to learn he was only five years old. He told her: "I'm a professor. I'm highly educated. Your little boy *really* believes there is another life after this. He really believes it, doesn't he? All my life, and that's a long time, I've believed I was an atheist. But this little boy has made me want to go back and reconsider my philosophy."

And that kind of impact is felt by all who are in the presence of Hans today.

He knows that he can act for himself and not be acted upon. Yes, he has severe limitations, but he takes full advantage of all the possibilities.

He just got his new electric power chair so he can pass the sacrament. He's writing a book. He can't do some things boys his age can do, which is hard for him—he admits that. But he is so very grateful for all he can do and takes joy in his abilities. He told me: "I'm a really good writer. And I have a really good ability to speak like an adult. And one more thing. I know there is another blessing the Lord will give me. I will have the opportunity to go on a mission. Somewhere, sometime, I will be able to go. It may not be a full-time mission, but I can go."

Hans chose greatness before he came. He is choosing to act and not be acted upon. Hans, my little friend, is a great and noble man, a giant among us all, and I have drunk deeply from his cup of lemonade.

One of the primary aims of science is to discover the laws that govern the natural world. When scientists discover these higher laws and obey them, marvelous things can happen. Men frontiering and adventuring into outer space is an example of the importance of obedience to laws.

Just as success, growth, and progress come from obedience to physical laws, so it is with spiritual laws. Obedience is a source of power. Obedience brings meekness, meekness brings the Holy Ghost, and the Holy Ghost "speaketh the truth and lieth not. Wherefore, it speaketh of things as they really are, and of things as they really will be" (Jacob 4:13), which "truth shall make you free" (John 8:32).

Whether that truth is a doctrinal issue, the solution to a business problem, needed insight in overcoming a serious weakness or sin, or understanding the potential in our personal relationships, truth given by the Holy Ghost will help us be free "to act . . . and not to be acted upon" (2 Nephi 2:26).

I have felt the least freedom in my life when I have tried so hard to hold on to my independence. Fear then replaces confidence, and fear always keeps us from being free. Sometimes we mortals feel that obedience means compulsion. Actually, obedience to God can be the ultimate witness of independence. Our agency, our freedom to choose for ourselves, is the one thing he absolutely will not take away from us. We really, truly are free to choose for ourselves. Thus, it is a tremendous witness of independence to be obedient to the Lord.

And what freedom do we gain from this? When we submit our wills to God, he will give back to us freedoms we can hardly comprehend. We will, through the Holy Ghost, have freedom to feel more with our hearts, know more with our minds, do more with our activities. And one more important thing—we will have the freedom to become the man or woman we truly want to be. We will be free to make better and sustained choices that will move us closer and closer to becoming Christlike.

I visited with a man who recently has lost a great deal of weight. His doctor had been advising him for some time to do just that, but he couldn't seem to get motivated. This time, however, he was animated as he told me of his success after sustained determination to succeed. It was so apparent as he talked that he felt better, healthier, and more at peace.

He told me that for years he had constantly struggled with the choice of whether to eat the dessert, the extra serving of potatoes, the fried foods, or the super double cheeseburger.

The heavier he grew, the less he tried. Exercise was a thing of the past—it required too much effort with his added burden. He didn't feel good physically or emotionally, and he always felt guilty, especially at mealtime.

He said that one evening in the temple the Spirit touched him, telling him that his appetites should be inside the Lord's boundaries. He realized he had been using lots and lots of excuses for being overweight and staying that way. He left the temple determined to choose good, choose more wisely, choose by obeying the laws of the body, and choose by listening to the Spirit.

He got out his library card. He found books to help him better understand the human body; he learned words like *fat grams* and *aerobic*. And the most important thing he did, even though he still didn't feel good about himself, was to choose to exercise every day and to not eat food overloaded in fat and calories.

He lost the weight and regained his health and increased stamina in dealing with life. He also lost the guilt, and he gained some knowledge about himself. He learned he was a person of discipline and power, that he could act for himself and not be acted upon. He learned that self-mastery comes from obedience. It wasn't the weight loss that made him look so happy and peaceful, it was that insight he had discovered as to his true greatness.

Our existence is governed by laws. It always has been and it always will be. God is God because he is *perfect* in his obedience to all the laws.

These rules, these parameters, surround us and envelop us completely. Many of these laws serve to protect us. Without laws, driving a car would be a ride in chaos and terror. Without laws, living in a community would be like living with street gangs. Without the laws of gravity, this earth could not exist. No one could learn, let alone master, a sport without obeying the laws that apply to it. Without abiding within the parameters of rules there would be no farms, no electricity, no plumbing, no organization, no industry, no education, and on and on and on. You see the picture. We are all obedient in some degree to many, many rules.

Those individuals who learn to obey more rules learn that they are able to acquire more knowledge and skills that make them successful. As an employer I have seen this over and over. I have had in my employ those who have had vast knowledge and skills in design and architecture, but who use other people's weaknesses, circumstances, or conditions around them to blame for their own failure to be accurate, meet a deadline, or solve problems. These people limit their progress because they can't be used in leadership positions. On the contrary, I have had entry-level designers and architects with very little knowledge and skills rise quickly to greater levels of trust and responsibility. When they have been faced with a problem to solve or a task to perform, they have never come back to the supervisor with anything but a task completed and the problem solved.

One year we had a most difficult project—upgrading a one-million-dollar residence into a three-million-dollar residence. Remodels are always difficult, but of this magnitude they are especially labor intensive for the designer and the client. To complicate matters, the clients were not willing to move out while the process took place. As the months unfolded, the clients wore out.

We wanted to be finished by Thanksgiving: the deadline was set, and the clients expected us to meet it. Fortunately we were able to finish construction well before the deadline. Even the floor coverings and window coverings were complete and installed. However, the furniture, art, and accessories would arrive only within a week of Thanksgiving.

Then disaster happened. A trucking strike immobilized all transportation to and from Los Angeles. The nonunion trucking companies were swamped with work. Our vendors, scattered all over southern California, informed us there was no way we would receive our orders. The junior designer on this job had only been out of college a few months. She had no experience as either a working designer or a project manager. Her supervisor told her there was no possible way to get the furniture here in time. This young girl decided not to "be acted upon." She came to me a few days later and said that the furniture would be arriving on schedule, as planned, for our installation.

I was amazed. She told me that she called someone she knew in Los Angeles to send her the city's yellow pages. She called all the trucking firms listed and found out that indeed, all were overloaded with work. So she called all the independent freight lines in Las Vegas and gathered costs to have them go down there and return to us. The costs were three times the budgeted amounts. So she called our vendors in California to find out their exact locations and driving times between each city. She estimated how big a truck would be required to carry all the goods. She called local do-it-yourself truck companies and estimated mileage, gas, distance, rental fees, and the like.

She knew she had to find a driver she could trust. She appealed to her college-age brother to do it and then also find a qualified student to assist. To meet their class schedules, the drivers could only pick up the items on Friday. She provided them with a detailed set of instructions from time of departure in Las Vegas to each factory, including estimated traveling times and the estimated time of return.

The furniture arrived as scheduled. The installation crew met the truck, and the client was well pleased with the results.

This young woman rose quickly in the company because she knew how to act, and not wait to be acted upon.

Recently I visited with a couple of individuals who have stonewalled their personal growth by pinning their fears or attitudes on "the way they were raised." Both of them came from homes where love was lost or abandoned. One of them came through the Depression. The other came through serious poverty. For both, childhood was filled with insecurity.

They have now lived a substantial amount of years. They have had good jobs, been able to provide very well for their families, and had great opportunities to serve in the Church. Both have benefited and grown tremendously from where they began life.

So why would they pull an old crutch that hasn't been used for years out of a dark closet and now use it to excuse behavior that holds them back? I don't know. I don't even think "why" is important. The Lord doesn't seem to discuss or direct us to look for reasons; he simply directs us to be obedient to principles.

Obedience makes us meek. And meekness is a requirement of self-mastery and overcoming the stumbling blocks of personal growth, including those we don't completely understand.

Elder Neal A. Maxwell wrote the following about the power of those who are meek: "Their obedience will see them through when reason and past experiences, by themselves, are not enough to sustain them. . . . It is a heroic thing for individuals to reverse themselves, their attitudes, and their patterns of behavior in order to pursue discipleship. . . .

"Self-control depends upon meekness. Otherwise, 'an angry man stirreth up strife, and a furious man aboundeth in transgression.' (Proverbs 29:22.) A furious man is out of control. Individuals who are meek may not always decipher what is happening to them or around them; however, even though they do not 'know the meaning of all things,' they know the Lord loves them. (1 Nephi 11:17.) They may feel overwhelmed, but they are not out of control" (*Meek and Lowly* [Salt Lake City: Deseret Book Co., 1987], pp. 55–56).

"For behold, it is not meet that I should command in all things; for he that is compelled in all things, the same is a slothful and not a wise servant; wherefore he receiveth no reward. Verily I say, men should be anxiously engaged in a good cause, and do many things of their own free will, and bring to pass much righteousness; for the power is in them, wherein they are agents unto themselves" (D&C 26–28).

My greatest struggle in growing up was to feel my individual worth. I had no sense, absolutely no sense at all, of my potential greatness. I believed becoming a great woman was not in my realm of possibility. Some of my early choices in life reflect that view of myself. My disobedience only made things worse. On the other hand, obedience always has been the way my self-esteem and view of possibility have been strengthened.

Satan wants desperately to grab hold of our hearts and whisper to us a spirit of fear. Among his counterfeits and half truths, he would show us things as they really are *not*. He would lull us and lead us away in our pride toward a false independence and no freedom at all.

We are not free at all when we sideswipe ourselves with language that reminds us of our disadvantages, weaknesses, or past histories of difficulties or sins. We are not free when our inappropriate behavior is blamed on other people's weaknesses or on conditions and circumstances beyond our control. We are not free when we search for self-esteem through our physical appearance, academic degrees, career status, or even perfect parenting. We are not free when we allow ourselves to be immobilized by our insecurities and withhold love, generosity, and service from God and our fellowmen.

If we are obedient, even though we act only out of duty, the Spirit will come. The Holy Ghost will visit us. He will stir us with the truth, and freedom will come. "The Spirit speaketh the truth, and lieth not" (Jacob 4:13). It is the truth, not just facts, that will make us free.

One of those truths is that even though our behavior doesn't always match our desire for greatness and our sincere quest for discipleship, the Savior is our Redeemer. And even though most of us are not behavioral scientists, repentance in the name of Jesus Christ offers us a chance to study and improve our behavior. We can, through repentance, ask the Lord to show us what we can do to be a part of the solution and not the problem. We can ask for inspiration to show us our part in making change.

President Ezra Taft Benson stated: "The Lord works from the

inside out. The world works from the outside in. The world would take people out of the slums. Christ takes the slums out of the people, and then they take themselves out of the slums. . . . Christ changes men, who then change their environment. The world would shape human behavior, but Christ can change human nature" ("Born of God," *Ensign*, Nov. 1985, p. 6).

Another one of those truths is that the Lord did not put us here to fail. In fact, he sent us a message through the ages, throughout all time, when he placed an angel to guard the tree of life in the Garden of Eden.

It seems likely that Adam and Eve had been eating of that tree the whole time they were in the garden. They were accustomed to it. It must have been delicious. When they fell after eating from the only tree forbidden and off limits, they might have been tempted to eat from the tree of life. If they had done that they would have lived forever in their sins without a savior.

The Lord protected them from being tempted beyond their power to resist when he guarded the pitfall with an angel and a flaming sword (see Moses 4:31). I believe we all have angels to guard us away from the way of destruction in our lives. They may not be literal angels, but I believe this record clearly testifies to us of God's great love and his concern for each of us to succeed. He stretches out his arm to us constantly to protect us. In our freedom to act and not be acted upon, unseen cherubim, whether figurative or literal, guard the way and thus can prevent us from being destroyed by conditions beyond our control.

And another truth is that we can have, through obedience, the companionship of the Holy Ghost, who will be our private tutor and teach us about real freedom. We can have more freedom from the natural man; freedom from the wiles of the devil; freedom from the things of the world; freedom from guilt, fears, and weaknesses; freedom to see we are becoming great men and great women.

The quest for greatness began long ago. We are traveling through this wilderness for that greatness at the journey's end.

Remember Alice in Wonderland?

Alice came to a junction that branched off in different directions and asked the Cheshire Cat for advice. The dialogue went something like this:

"Would you please tell me which way I ought to go from here?"

"That depends a good deal on where you want to get to from here," said the cat.

"I don't much care where," said Alice.

"Then it doesn't much matter which way you go," said the cat.

The New Testament speaks of some would-be great men and great women who found it too difficult to continue in their journey. When the Savior completed his sermon in Capernaum, many of his disciples murmured, said it was too difficult, and abandoned him: "From that time many of his disciples went back, and walked no more with him. Then said Jesus unto the twelve, Will ye also go away? Then Simon Peter answered him, Lord, to whom shall we go? thou hast the words of eternal life" (John 6:66–68).

In other words, there is only one way to true greatness, and that is the Savior. He is the Way.

I have self-esteem. I believe that I am of great worth and that someday I can become the woman I really want to be. I have struggled in this quest, like a chick hatching from its shell.

But I am also only a few weeks away from losing it. If I stop trying to be obedient; if I start watching R-rated movies, neglect my prayers, and dismiss the need of daily, sincere repentance; if I forget the scriptures, dishonor the Sabbath day regularly, and so on, then some morning I might wake up depressed, full of doubt and despair.

I am ordinary. I make no pretense at perfection. But I am trying, and I bear witness that the gospel gives us our only chance to true greatness.

Remember: obedience to the commandments renders us meek. Meekness invites the Holy Ghost, who can teach us more and inspire us with love—love of God, love for God, and love for ourselves and each other.

Through obedience to the principles of the gospel we find out the most important information about ourselves we can ever know. The number one reason for being obedient is to find out that we love the Lord, that we have always loved him, that he loves us, and that he has always loved us.

I can't remember when my quest for greatness began. But when I choose wisely, correctly, and justly, the Spirit confirms that I am free to act for myself and not be acted upon. The Spirit also comforts me that, even though I can't remember, I somehow do know my quest for greatness began long, long ago. And it began with the words, "Thou mayest choose for thyself."

CHAPTER THREE

"And On, On to the Victory"

There came an hour in Elder Spencer W. Kimball's life when he had to find courage to understand his greatness.

Immediately after he received his call to the apostleship, he began to be filled with self-doubt and feelings of great weakness. For six days and nights he suffered. He began to think about all the times he had offended someone or had had misunderstandings with others. He felt he had been petty and small in so many things. In his own words:

"Hot tears came flooding down my cheeks as I made no effort to mop them up. I was accusing myself, and condemning myself and upbraiding myself. I was praying aloud for special blessings from the Lord. . . . I did not spare myself. A thousand things passed through my mind. Was I called by revelation? Or, had the Brethren been impressed by the recent contacts in my home and stake when they had visited us, or by the accounts of my work in the flood rehabilitation which reports I knew had been greatly exaggerated in my favor? Had I been called because of my relationship to one of the First Presidency?"

He yearned and prayed for the assurance that his call had been inspired. He felt if that witness would come, many of his doubts would be subdued.

"I knew full well that He knew all the imperfections of my life and He knew my heart. And I knew that I must have His acceptance before I could go on. I stumbled up the hill and onto the mountain, as the way became rough. . . . I climbed on and on. Never had I prayed before as I now prayed. What I wanted and felt I must have was an assurance that I was acceptable to the Lord. . . . I wanted only the calm peaceful assurance that my offering was accepted. Never before had I been tortured as I was now being tortured. And the assurance did not come" (Edward L. Kimball and Andrew E. Kimball, Jr., *Spencer W. Kimball* [Salt Lake City: Bookcraft, 1977], pp. 193–94).

Of course, eventually, the assurance came, but not without his first experiencing the loneliness.

If at first your prayers don't always seem answered, take heart. One greater than you or I or President Kimball cried out, "My God, my God, why hast thou forsaken me?" (Matthew 27:46).

If for a while the harder you try, the harder it gets, remember that it has been so with the greatest men and greatest women who have ever lived. Men like Noah, Abraham, Joseph, Job, Paul, Joseph Smith, and my friend Hans. Women like Ruth, Hannah, Esther, Abish, Emma, those who walked the plains, and my friend Selma, whom I will discuss later in this chapter. Great men and great women who pressed on with courage to be victorious.

We came into this world for the victory. Victory means success over an opponent or opposition. We always talk about the War in Heaven as if it is a distant and removed event to which we are no longer connected. That war continues here. We are very much in the throes of it. Satan battles for our souls, for our demise. He fights against the Savior. The battlefield has changed, but the war continues.

Remember Winston Churchill's great address on 13 May 1940? The Nazi army was threatening the English Channel and subsequent invasion to the British Isles. Prime Minister Churchill went before the House of Commons and with soberness but great valor said these words: "We have before us an ordeal of the most grievous kind. We have before us many, many long months of struggle and of suffering. You ask what is our policy? I will say: It is to wage war, by sea, land and air, with all our might and with all our strength that God can give us. . . . You ask, What is our aim? I can answer in one word: Victory—victory at all costs, victory in spite of all terror, victory, however long and hard the road may be" (*Churchill: The Life Triumphant* [New York: American Heritage, 1965], p. 90).

It is to wage war that we were born into this world. The Lord counsels us to "put on the whole armour of God, that ye may be able to stand against the wiles of the devil" (Ephesians 6:11). We came to battle for our lives, our eternal lives. No matter how long and hard the road, we came here to be victorious!

We cannot let our armor be discarded or removed in moments of weakness. Whether that weakness be from sin or sorrow, we must never allow ourselves to lose hope. We cannot allow our swords of hope to be thrust into a furnace of despair, or we will find ourselves with a useless and misshapen weapon.

There is not a single person reading this who has not had to muster courage a time or two in their lives. And probably for some, a great deal of courage. There may be those who are reading these words because they are seeking strength. Certainly all of us, in a coming day, will have another trial in which our courage will be needed in order for us to be victorious.

What has victory come to mean to you? For me it has not meant any significant accomplishment that has brought attention or accolades. There have been some public victories, yes, but they are small and insignificant when I weigh them in the balance with the joy that private victories have brought to me.

The private victories of our lives are as individual and personal as the stars are numerous. But the results of those victories are universal. These victories bring a special kind of joy and peace into our lives.

I was not alive when World War II ended, but I have read the accounts, seen the films, and talked at length with family and friends who were. There was such a joy to have won the war and have the hardship over. There was a joy and peace throughout the world. Loved ones were reunited, new families were created, economies started progressing, and renewed gratitude for life filled the world.

Victory in our personal lives means freedom from fears. It means peace and joy in our everyday, ordinary work of mortal life. And it means a more tender gratitude for who we are and who we can become. It means a deepening appreciation of the Savior's atonement and his role in our daily lives.

My worldly accomplishments and acquisitions are insignificant to me, and spiritual victories have come to mean everything! One reason why they mean so much is that the war is *not* over with each victory. I will wage this war until I draw my last breath of life. We will be victorious, you and I, but only if we press forward and realize that we came to work hard. Our successes will be based on our choices along the way, both good and bad; developed from obedience, or lack of it; built upon our stretch for faith or faltering from time to time; and molded from experience, either weakened by those experiences we simply lived through or strengthened by those we worked through.

Engaging in a little wordplay, we might look at the term *battle sword* and notice that by moving one letter, we get *battle words*. I would like to lend you six words to help you in the battles of life. They are, in a manner of speaking, six battle swords of courage. They will, when grasped with a steady hand of hope, give us strength to endure to the end. No, they will not eliminate trails and sorrows and difficulties. But they absolutely will, when lifted with faith and hope, strengthen us against the opposition. They will deliver you and me to the victory! They are *press, perspective, purpose, patience, prayer,* and *Paul.*

How can mere words really help us? One way is to draw on the power of memory. In those darker hours of life we still have choices. We can lie in the dark and dwell on all the turmoil and sorrow, or we can open the door to more light by pondering thoughts that will strengthen us, thoughts that include the Savior. To recall or remember a word like *patience* or *press* can be an instant opening to dwelling on better thoughts. Thus words can become a sword that slices through mists of darkness. There are many such words in the scriptures; these are only meant to suggest a process.

The first battle sword is *press.* In the English language the word *press* means many things; it is both a noun and a verb. We want to use it both ways in this victory effort. As a verb we use it to mean "push forward, push against, or squeeze tightly."

Usually we press against something because there is a force of resistance. It is indeed a symbolic word of battle, as Paul said, "I press toward the mark for the prize of the high calling of God in Christ Jesus" (Philippians 3:14). Paul understood this word. He knew its meaning and was inspired with the spirit of that meaning. Paul had "suffered the loss of all things" in his quest for greatness, but pressed forward that he "may win Christ" (Philippians 3:8).

Paul was well acquainted with the press *against* him, yet he pressed *forward* with a determination to righteously hang on.

Elder Neal A. Maxwell wrote: "One cannot be laid back and still press forward. To 'awake to righteousness' requires us to 'awake and arouse [our] faculties' and to 'awake to a remembrance' and to dispel the 'cloud of darkness,' so that we, like

Lamoni, can be 'lit up in [the] soul'" (*A Wonderful Flood of Light* [Salt Lake City: Bookcraft, 1990], p. 83).

Had Paul ceased pressing forward, he may well have become un-pressed or de-pressed, and then his life would have been a different story. De-pressing is what grieves our current, ailing generation. Many are sick in spirit with depression, a despair of giving up that shrouds all hope.

Nephi saw many of us "pressing forward" toward the tree of eternal life. And even through the mists of darkness (symbolic of our fears and trials and sorrow) "they did press their way forward, continually holding fast to the rod of iron, until they came forth and fell down and partook of the fruit of the tree" (1 Nephi 8:30). "Fell down" might suggest how hard the battle for victory was fought. It might mean "overcome with joy at having achieved the victory." Whatever it represents to each of us, the result is universal to those who press on and never give up. It is the making of great men and great women.

If we use the word *press* as a noun, there is only one word that captures the fulness of this unique and individual victory. That word is *winepress*, which is the English translation of the Hebrew word for Gethsemane.

There in that sacred garden setting came the most exquisite and painful press toward greatness the world will ever know. Upon this press hinges the greatness of all mankind. The force of suffering so multiplied by the sins and sorrows of "every kind" and "the pains and sicknesses of his people" caused the great Jehovah to bleed from every pore (Alma 7:11).

I met Selma on my second day at BYU. I was assigned a room on the third floor of one of the Helaman Hall dormitories. Most of us on that floor were entering freshmen, and some of us had come from states far away. Selma had come from North Carolina, and she had a little southern drawl that drew a crowd. I remember never tiring of hearing her say, "Budge Hall"—it came out like "Boodge." We gathered around her often and loved to be entertained by her charming accent and terrific personality. She never complained about the coaxing, "Come on, Selma; say 'Boodge' one more time!" She was a great sport and a great friend. She was also a talented musician who had come to BYU on a full-ride music scholarship.

We were part of a large friendship that has endured after graduation, marriage, and families. We have kept in touch, including reunions over the years. We all knew of Selma's battle for victory. She had since childhood struggled to survive with diabetes.

She was a wife and mother of two teenage sons when she died at the age of forty. She had become blind and had endured much illness and several amputations. She was no longer able to teach or play the piano. She was suffering the ravages of the disease physically, but spiritually Selma was winning the battle with uncommon valor.

I spoke to her the night before she was to have an amputation to remove another limb from her body. Her voice was so weak that she could hardly talk above a whisper. I asked her what she needed. I told her that I wanted to take care of something, anything that she needed to do but couldn't. Her reply to me was the proof that my friend Selma is a great woman. In a whispering voice with that familiar soft drawl, she said, "Anita, I lay here in this hospital bed so extremely grateful for my life. I love the Savior. I love this church. I have a wonderful temple marriage, two wonderful sons, righteous parents who taught me the gospel, and a husband who is my best friend. My life is full; it is complete. The Savior has been with me year after year. It has been a joy to have had the Holy Ghost in my life as a companion, a teacher, and, especially through this disease, a comforter. I have never doubted God's love for me, and I have a lot of patience with this affliction. I have suffered physical pain, but I have endured faithfully. Now my pain is different. My husband and sons and my parents stood tonight at the foot of this bed, and even though I couldn't see them I felt their sorrow. I felt their suffering for me. No matter that I tell them that I am okay—I feel their tremendous pain.

"Anita, there is something you can do. You can pray for my family to be comforted. And you can pray for me and ask the Lord if my life is acceptable to him, will he take me home—tonight—before the surgery in the morning, so that my family can have peace and rest. I don't want to ask for anything against his will. I will endure to whenever he says the end is. I just want my family to have peace."

That night many of Selma's friends sent her message home to the Father and asked that his will be done. Her life was indeed acceptable to him. She did not wake up. She and her family were spared another horrendous amputation. She slipped away in her sleep. She had never given up. She had *pressed* toward the mark and she was victorious!

The second battle sword is *perspective.*

Proper perspective is one of the key ingredients of having courage to endure our trials and tribulations and become greater men and women: "Even so I would that ye should do in all holiness of heart, walking uprightly before me, considering the end of your salvation, doing all things with prayer and thanksgiving" (D&C 46:7).

"Considering the end or your salvation" is to look forward with an eye of faith and keep the bigger picture in mind.

President Spencer W. Kimball wrote: "The Lord is omnipotent, with all power to control our lives, save us pain, prevent all accidents, drive all planes and cars, feed us, protect us, save us from labor, effort, sickness, even from death, if He will, but He will not. We should be able to understand this, because we can realize how unwise it would be for us to shield our children from all effort, from disappointments, sorrows, and suffering. . . .

"If we looked at mortality as the whole of existence, then pain, sorrow, failure, and short life would be a calamity. But if we look upon life as an eternal thing stretching far into the pre-earth past and on into the eternal post-death future, then all happenings may be put in proper perspective" (*Tragedy or Destiny* [Salt Lake City: Deseret Book Co, 1977], p. 2).

Many years ago my husband decided to fulfill his dream of being a dentist. Together we made the decision we should do this. At age thirty-three that meant he would have to embark on a five-year program as a full-time student. We had four children, a beautiful custom home, and a successful business. It would mean tremendous sacrifices. There were many around us who wondered if we were losing our minds. But there were many more who were delighted and supportive of this career change for him. However, one individual seemed intent on casting doubts into our minds as to whether we were stable people! His remarks were often sarcastic and condemning. I watched Steve always respond positively and generously to this person. But it was so uncomfortable that we dreaded meeting him in the hallway at church.

Finally one day he began needling Steve again, and when he couldn't get a negative response he blurted out, "Well, how *old* will you be when you get out of dental school?" To which Steve quickly said, "The same age I'll be if I don't go to dental school!" In other words, he would be thirty-eight whether he went or not, and if he went he'd be thirty-eight *and* a dentist.

That is perspective!

Throughout those five years, we had a great time. We got to live in the San Francisco Bay area. We made lifelong friends in our ward. We enjoyed the culture and beauty of California.

Sometimes others would sympathetically say, "You are changing careers—wow, we sympathize with what you must be going through." We didn't see it that way. We both look back on those years with so much enjoyment. I would do it again. And now Steve is a dentist and established in a successful practice. It was all worth it. Was it a piece of cake? Of course not. It was hard, at times very, very hard. During those years our oldest son left home to embark on a path of drugs and alcohol, a troubled niece came to live with us, my extended family had serious problems, and I was the sole breadwinner. But there is a motto that Steve and I agreed to live by when we married. It goes like this: There Is Just As Much Joy in the Striving As There Is in the Arriving. In other words, if we wait for the trial, ordeal, or problem to end before we are going to be happy, we will miss the best parts of life.

Elder Neal A. Maxwell wrote: "To err by having naive expectations concerning the purposes of life is to err everlastingly. Life is neither a pleasure palace through whose narrow portals we pass briefly, laughingly, and heedlessly before extinction, nor a cruel predicament in an immense and sad wasteland. It is the middle (but briefest) and proving state of the three estates in man's carefully constructed continuum of experience.

"One day we will understand fully how complete our commitment was in our first estate in accepting the very conditions of challenge in our second estate about which we sometimes complain in this school of stress. Our collective and personal premortal promises will then be laid clearly before us" (*All These Things Shall Give Thee Experience* [Salt Lake City: Deseret Book Co., 1980], p. 47).

He further taught that "correct conduct under stress is more likely when one has correct expectations about life" (ibid.). To have proper perspective and correct expectations we have to do three things. We have to (1) trust in the Lord, (2) be of good cheer, and (3) look forward always.

"But straightway Jesus spake unto them, saying, Be of good cheer; it is I; be not afraid. And Peter answered him and said, Lord, if it be thou, bid me come unto thee on the water. And he said, Come. And when Peter was come down out of the ship, he walked on the water, to go to Jesus. But when he saw the wind boisterous, he was afraid; and beginning to sink, he cried, saying, Lord, save me. And immediately Jesus stretched forth his hand, and caught him, and said unto him, O thou of little faith, wherefore didst thou doubt?" (Matthew 14:27–31).

Peter hearkened to the Savior's council to be of good cheer even though the storm was scary and the water rough. He asked the Savior to bid him come to him on the water, thus demonstrating his trust in the Lord. He looked forward "to go to Jesus," but when he allowed himself to focus on the storm, looking away instead of forward, he began to sink.

To trust in the Lord is to be humble enough to have simple trust. God created this world: he commands the elements and forces of nature, he established order in the universe, he has a plan. We are part of that plan. If we are obedient and repent faithfully we can feel assured we are watched over. I do not understand all the calamities, difficulties, and trials that beset me, but I do know there is a plan and that God loves me. He understands our need to be stretched so that we can deepen spiritually and strengthen discipleship. Membership alone in this Church does not constitute discipleship. Discipleship is striving to emulate the Lord. I do not know how to do this by myself. I need experiences to help me learn how to be more Christlike. I need to trust in the Lord.

In this regard, C. S. Lewis wrote: "I find I must borrow yet another parable from George MacDonald. Imagine yourself as a

living house. God comes in to rebuild that house. At first, perhaps, you can understand what He is doing. He is getting the
drains right and stopping the leaks in the roof and so on: you
knew that those jobs needed doing and so you are not surprised.
But presently, He starts knocking the house about in a way that
hurts abominably and does not seem to make sense. What on
earth is He up to? The explanation is that He is building quite a
different house from the one you thought of—throwing out a
new wing here, putting on an extra floor there, running up
towers, making courtyards. You thought you were going to be
made into a decent little cottage: but He is building a palace"
(*Mere Christianity* [New York: Macmillan, 1960], p. 174).

I love the simple trust of children in a God they hardly understand. When my son and his cousin Abe were both eight years old
they went on a Saturday afternoon bicycle adventure in the
desert. They played too long and realized they weren't going to
get home before dusk. It was a moonless night and darkness soon
enveloped them. Not far from home, Abe's bike chain broke.
They began to feel frightened and worried about the vagrants
known to live in this particular area. Then they thought they
heard muffled voices. They considered abandoning their bikes
and running, but decided that would be a mistake—home was too
far and they were too vulnerable. Suddenly they both knew what
to do. Abe said, "Heavenly Father can fix my chain." So with a
simple trust they knelt in the dirt and asked him to help them.
Chase reached out to touch the chain, and it seemed to snap
easily in place. In amazement and gratitude they jumped on the
bikes and came safely home to report of their great experience.

Why do we become so jaded as we become older that we lose
that trust?

I believe it's usually because of pride. It's usually because we
murmur and complain, "Oh great, my bike chain broke again! I

refuse to stand this any longer," or something like that. This was the distinct difference between Laman and Lemuel and their brother Nephi. Eventually Laman and Lemuel couldn't be trusted, but it began because they did not trust God. "They did murmur in many things against their father, because he was a visionary man, and had led them out of the land of Jerusalem, to leave the land of their inheritance, and their gold, and their silver, and their precious things, to perish in the wilderness. . . . And thus Laman and Lemuel, being the eldest, did murmur against their father. And they did murmur because they knew not the dealings of that God who had created them" (1 Nephi 2:11–12).

Emma Smith murmured because she wanted to participate in the translation, she wanted to see the ancient records, she felt left out. The Lord revealed to her the antidote for murmuring: "Murmur not because of the things which thou hast not seen, for they are withheld from thee and from the world, which is wisdom in men in a time to come. And the office of thy calling shall be for a comfort unto my servant, Joseph Smith, Jun., thy husband, in his afflictions, with consoling words, in the spirit of meekness. . . . Continue in the spirit of meekness, and beware of pride" (D&C 25:4–5, 14).

To be of good cheer means to choose to find as much joy in the striving as in the arriving. It does not mean we won't have sorrow or that we must have a Pollyanna mentality. Being of good cheer is demonstrating that we feel secure in the Lord's plans even though our plans are full of disappointment. It is a vital part of perspective. If we have unrealistic expectations about life, we will miss that larger eternal view while the narrower mortal view overwhelms us. Elder Neal A. Maxwell has written: "Two of the basic things over which we are to be justifiably of good cheer are the transcendent blessings that our sins are forgiven and that Jesus has overcome the world. Additionally, we are assured that He is in our midst, He will lead us along, and He will stand by us. . . . Therefore, knowing that these major and everlasting things are in place, we can better endure such mundane trials as a frustrating traffic jam. And at those times we can be calm enough to ask ourselves how it can rain on the just and the unjust alike (Matt. 5:45) without occasionally raining on our parade" (*A Wonderful Flood of Light*, p. 66). Being of good cheer is changing our focus so that our perspective becomes a deeper, broader view.

Anne Marie Rose was an energetic, athletic teenager filled with commitment to see her hopes and expectations materialize. She trained for months to become a member of her school's varsity volleyball team. She ran, lifted weights, spent hours doing the drills. She made the team and was on her way, or so she thought. She soon saw that others played better than she. She spent most of the game time on the bench, dealing with her disappointment. Her attitude began to change, and it began to affect her relationship with the other girls. She said: "Why would Heavenly Father let me work so hard and come so far to end up so disappointed? . . . I decided to leave the team. I needed to get back to my studies and my life away from volleyball.

"But I couldn't seem to let go of my disappointment and resentment. Then general conference came."

At that conference President Gordon B. Hinckley spoke of the emigration of thousands of European Saints who faced their trials and disappointments with not only optimism but also enthusiasm. He counseled all of us to do likewise. Anne Marie was touched. Perspective returned. She continued:

"President Hinckley's address offered the counsel I needed to put things into perspective. By having an 'overpowering spirit of optimism' and enthusiasm (*Ensign*, Nov. 1995, p. 72), I could *decide* to let go of my volleyball experience. I could *decide* to be positive and optimistic about the many good things in my life: my friendships, my studies, my family. I could play volleyball for *fun* rather than competition. Suddenly the dilemma that had seemed so overwhelming began to fade. I started to feel better about myself. I read the scriptures more. I prayed more. I liked other people more. I felt the Spirit reenter my life.

"I am grateful for a living prophet who taught me to let go of feeling sorry for myself. He quoted Alma 26:35, which teaches us there never was a people 'that had so great reason to rejoice as we, since the world began.' I realize now that I have so much to be grateful for, so many reasons to rejoice" ("Facing Trials with Optimism," *Ensign*, May 1996, p. 87).

To look forward always is to do what Peter didn't do. We should never take our eyes off the Savior, for he is the way home, especially during storms of distraction. Elder Maxwell taught: "Lacking gospel light or ignoring gospel perspective, we create many of our own problems. Those who desire complexity instead of simplicity can surely complicate simple things. Those who insist on 'looking beyond the mark'—the obvious—are those most likely to trip over stumbling blocks, as the Jews were anciently: 'But behold, the Jews were a stiffnecked people; and they despised the words of plainness, and killed the prophets, and sought for things that they could not understand. Wherefore, because of their blindness, which blindness came by looking beyond the mark, they must needs fall'. . . (Jacob 4:14)" (*A Wonderful Flood of Light*, p. 82).

To have perspective we must keep our lens sharply focused on our path of duty—on the Savior—so that we will not be distracted by money, clothes, good looks, talents, careers, honors and praise of men, intellect, recreation, sins, or trials and tribulations. So that we need not fall.

To continue in the faith of what we have been taught about the Second Coming is also looking forward. Looking forward is imagining ourselves already where we want to be and then walking down the road that leads to the Savior's door.

"Do ye exercise faith in the redemption of him who created you? Do you *look forward* with an eye of faith, and view this mortal body raised in immortality, and this corruption raised in incorruption. . . . I say unto you, can you *imagine to yourselves* that ye hear the voice of the Lord, saying unto you, in that day: Come unto me ye blessed, for behold, your works have been the works of righteousness upon the face of the earth?" (Alma 5:15–16; emphasis added).

To look forward is to emulate the Savior's example.

"And it came to pass, when the time was come that he should be received up, he *stedfastly set his face to go to Jerusalem*" (Luke 9:51; emphasis added). In other words, he looked towards Jerusalem with great commitment and determination. He knew what awaited him there. But he never looked away or looked back when it was time for him to "be received up."

One evening in the Las Vegas Temple I witnessed a victory, a special victory that had to be born from courage that comes from keeping one's eye looking forward, focused on the Savior.

It was an unusual session in the fact that there were several individuals present with various disabilities. For example, one woman's feet were in special bandages, perhaps from some sort of surgery. There was also an elderly gentleman who was deaf. A television with closed caption had been brought in and placed in the front of the room for him. But the person who seemed the most handicapped was a very young man, about the age of a missionary, who was using a walker and was also being assisted by a man who appeared to be his father.

This young man, not much more than a boy really, seemed to

struggle with each movement. He could not stand on his own and appeared to have tremendous difficulty in moving his limbs. I saw him a few days later at a wedding reception and learned who he was and what had happened to him.

He was a returned missionary. While snowboarding in Utah one Saturday, he had an accident that literally broke his neck. He was not supposed to live. In fact, there were some moments when his family thought he was indeed going to die. But he didn't. The prognosis was that he would never walk again. But he is walking. And I had the privilege of seeing where it was he wanted to walk to. He wanted to return to the temple.

That night in the temple, before I knew who he was, I watched his face. It seemed to me he was at such peace, a peace that surpassed his youth and his obviously painful ordeal. He looked so extremely happy to be there that night.

Near the end of the session, an invitation was extended to those who wanted to participate in the prayer circle. This young man was helped up on his walker by his father, and together they went up to the prayer circle. The television monitor had to be moved and a chair pushed aside to make room as he awkwardly made his way to the group. His father supported his arm and steadied the way.

Then I saw the special moment. Instead of joining the circle or returning to his seat, this loving father stepped behind his son. With both of his arms he reached out and wrapped them around his son's chest and under his arms. The boy let go of the walker so he could stand and participate in the prayer. His father threw his entire strength into holding up his son so that he could be a part of this beautiful occasion.

It was one of the most touching scenes I have ever seen—a vivid portrayal of how great the Savior's and the Father's love is for us.

This young man had been through a grievous ordeal, a personal stormy sea. But he had not allowed himself to be distracted by the winds of adversity; rather, he had focused firmly on the Savior. He had wanted to return to the temple as part of his goals. He was walking on the turbulent waters to "go to Jesus." He was walking!

I saw the victory and much more. I saw a sweet metaphor of our Savior's love. If we will look to him, he will be there. He will support us; he will encircle us and sustain us, even if we can't see him. He will always remember us.

If we aren't looking forward, we are looking back—and we won't ever be able to maintain perspective and see the greatness in ourselves.

The third battle sword is *purpose*. To have purpose means to accept the truth taught that we were born to be in the celestial kingdom. Stephen Robinson teaches that once we are baptized, we are already in the kingdom of God. We just have to learn to stay in it (see *Following Christ* [Salt Lake City: Deseret Book Co., 1995], pp. 6–7). We have a purpose here. It is to become like the Savior and eventually be joint heirs with him. If we can accept that truth, our victories will increase, especially the ones we battle emotionally and spiritually. If we can wield the sword of purpose, we change our questions of doubt into one great and final question to be asked of ourselves constantly, "How can I be more Christlike and what is my duty?"

To have *purpose* as a battle sword is to ask that question in a moment of contention, when facing any conflict, when enduring a trial, when being called upon to serve the Church or others, when confronted with personal weaknesses, when tempted, and when we sin.

To have *purpose* as a battle sword is to do three things—and really, they are the only three things we need to do in life. They are to obey, repent, and forgive.

A young man went to see Elder Marvin J. Ashton to be set

apart as a missionary. He came alone, without his parents, without friends. Elder Ashton asked him:

"'Is your father a member of the Church?'

"He said, 'No.'

"'Is your mother a member of the Church?'

"He responded with, 'Just barely.'

"I said, 'Does your father want you to go on a mission?'

"He answered, 'No.'

"'Does your mother want you to go on a mission?'

"'She really doesn't care whether I go or not.'

"'Well, why are you going?'

"'Just because I've always wanted to go and I think I can make a success of it.'

"I looked at that young man in the face and said, 'It seems to me you have two and one-half strikes against you, but from what I hear, and what I feel of your spirit, you will not strike out'" (*Murmur Not*, Brigham Young University Speeches of the Year [Provo, 9 Dec. 1969], pp. 5–6).

Elder Ashton observed that this was a great person who had the opportunity to murmur, "My dad doesn't care, my mother doesn't care, why should I?" Instead he chose to obey the prophet, make himself worthy to go, and forgive those who didn't support him in his good choices. This young man had purpose. He wanted to make a success of his mission and become the man he should be.

To obey with purpose means that we submit our will to the Lord's and choose to keep the commandments. No matter how "boisterous the wind," how full of distractions our lives can be, we are to just obey the Savior and go down the path of duty. It doesn't require perfection; it doesn't require total understanding; it doesn't even require that we agree. To obey with purpose is to love the Lord enough to just do it right.

To repent with purpose is to desire to be like him—in heart, in mind, in action. It is to pay attention to our words, deeds, and thoughts and to yearn to cleanse the inner vessel. It is to be grateful we have the Savior and his atonement.

To forgive with purpose is to emulate him, even as he exclaimed these unbelievable words from the cross: "Father, forgive them; for they know not what they do" (Luke 23:34). To forgive with purpose is to look for the beam in our own eye and not the mote in our brother's. It is to be meek and lowly, to love one another, and to esteem our neighbor as ourselves. It is to ultimately feel the divine power of godliness in our souls.

The fourth battle sword is *patience*. President Spencer W. Kimball wrote: "Being human, we would expel from our lives physical pain and mental anguish and assure ourselves of continual ease and comfort, but if we were to close the doors upon sorrow and distress, we might be excluding our greatest friends and benefactors. Suffering can make Saints of people, as they learn patience, long-suffering, and self-mastery" (*Faith Precedes the Miracle* [Salt Lake City: Deseret Book Co., 1972], p. 98).

Our historical records here on earth are replete with the heroic patience of individuals and collective groups of people. There have been vast numbers of the aged, poor, helpless, lonely, abandoned, abused, and scorned. We are not alone in our struggle for patience, but are we worthy to stand with those like Joseph of Egypt, Job, Hannah, Abraham, Joseph Smith, the pioneers who walked the plain, the Nazi death camp prisoners, or the many among us today affected by disease, divorce, and tragedy and yet who never murmur?

Elder Neal A. Maxwell shared some great insights that help us understand the battle sword of *patience* and how it matters for victory:

"Patience is tied very closely to faith in our Heavenly Father.

Actually, when we are unduly impatient we are suggesting that we know what is best—better than does God. Or, at least, we are asserting that our timetable is better than His. Either way we are questioning the reality of God's omniscience as if, as some seem to believe, God were on some sort of postdoctoral fellowship and were not quite in charge of everything. . . .

"Patience is a willingness, in a sense, to watch the unfolding purposes of God with a sense of wonder and awe, rather than pacing up and down within the cell of our circumstance. Put another way, too much anxious opening of the oven door and the cake falls instead of rising. So it is with us. If we are always selfishly taking our temperature to see if we are happy, we will not be. . . .

"I remember as a child going eagerly to the corner store for what we then called an 'all-day sucker.' It would not have lasted all day under the best usage, but it could last quite a while. The trick was to resist the temptation to bite into it, to learn to savor rather than to crunch and chew. The same savoring was needed with a precious square of Hershey milk chocolate to make the treat last, especially in depression times.

"In life, however, even patiently stretching out sweetness is sometimes not enough; in certain situations, enjoyment must actually be deferred. A patient willingness to defer dividends is a hallmark of individual maturity. . . .

"Clearly, without patience we will learn less in life. We will see less; we will feel less; we will hear less. Ironically, 'rush' and 'more' usually mean 'less.' The pressure of 'now,' time and time again, go against the grain of the gospel with its eternalism. . . .

"Patience is . . . clearly not fatalistic, shoulder-shrugging resignation. It is the acceptance of a divine rhythm to life; it is obedience prolonged. Patience stoutly resists pulling up the daisies to see how the roots are doing. Patience is never condescending or exclusive—it is never glad when others are left out. Patience never preens itself; it prefers keeping the window of the soul open" ("Patience," in *1979 Devotional Speeches of the Year* [Provo, Utah: Brigham Young University Press, 1980], pp. 215, 216, 217, 218–19).

Patience teaches us not only to endure but also to endure well and endure to the end. For example, the Nephites found themselves in severe bondage to the Lamanites and prayed for help. Though we do not know how long they were thus afflicted, we do know that the Lord heard their earnest pleadings. And we know how they then responded:

"The burdens which were laid upon Alma and his brethren were made light; yea, the Lord did strengthen them that they could bear up their burdens with ease, and they did submit cheerfully and with patience to all the will of the Lord.

"And it came to pass that so great was their faith and their patience that the voice of the Lord came unto them again, saying: Be of good comfort, for on the morrow I will deliver you out of bondage" (Mosiah 24:15–16).

Armed with cheerful patience they won the battle. They were victorious over both the Lamanites and the adversary.

The fifth battle sword is *prayer*. Prayer is a true sword for battle against the adversary. When we pray, were aren't giving the Lord any information he doesn't already have. He already knows about our problems, and he already knows about our joys and our gratitude. Prayer isn't for him. It's for us. That's why Hans told me Heavenly Father is picky in the way he wants us to talk to him.

In order for prayer to be a true weapon of power, we must be honest with God in order to be honest with ourselves. We must take time to truly talk to him so that he may speak to us. And we must take the time to worship him in this very private hour. We must use prayer as a means of growing closer to him.

Prayer is a commandment. There are different types of prayer, such as prayers of gratitude, of confession, of worship, of request for blessings. The Lord counsels us to pray over our work, our livelihood, our possessions, our food, our families, our fellowmen, and our enemies.

He promises us: "If thou shalt ask, thou shalt receive revelation upon revelation, knowledge upon knowledge, that thou mayest know the mysteries and peaceable things—that which bringeth joy, that which bringeth life eternal" (D&C 42:61).

To have peace in a world of sorrow is indeed a victory!

Our greatest challenge in learning to use prayer as a battle sword is to draw close enough to the Lord that we petition him according to his will, not ours.

Understanding this changes the way we pray. The Lord always provides a way for us to escape our trials. Of course, we have to be striving to keep the commandments. But there is something else we must realize. The delivery will almost never be *out* of the trial, but rather *through* it.

But how does this change the way we pray? Instead of continually pleading for deliverance, we now submit our will to his and ask what we can do: "What can I do to solve the problem?" "What action can I take?" "What wouldst thou have me do?" "What can I do to help others in need?" "How can I serve thee?"

My life changed when I began praying with and for more submissiveness. My prayers are not perfect by any means, and there are still times when I succumb to my will over his. But into my life have come more peace, more power, and more victory over ill as I have sought for that "which is right" in my prayers (see 3 Nephi 18:20). From time to time prayers of courage simply press against the adversity, simple words of "Heavenly Father, wilt thou strengthen me for the coming hour until I can stand it again?"

There are trials over which I have prayed that have gone on for years and are not yet resolved. Does this necessarily mean that he isn't listening or that Anita isn't worthy?

It certainly does not.

In fact, I feel closer to my Father as I have discussed these matters with him over the years. He is well acquainted with my thoughts and heartfelt desires. I have felt him listen, I have heard his counsel, I have learned from his wisdom, I have developed greater strength. I have felt his love. My faith has increased, my hope has brightened, and, the best gift of all, my love for others has deepened.

No, not all the trials have gone away, but the Lord has eased my burdens. I feel closer to him than I would have without these burdens. Prayer has led me to him.

When we are led to him, we are also led to the temple. We have been invited to come unto him and to learn of him. Where is he? Where would we find him, figuratively and literally? It is my witness that he is in his house. Within the walls of the temple, this house of learning, the Lord will teach us what we need to know to fortify ourselves against the raging war with the adversary.

The temple is a special house of worship and prayer. There we learn about prayer as in no other place. There we are reminded to call upon the Lord frequently and involve him in our lives.

The temple is a house of prayer. It is a place where we can regroup and muster courage to "go forth from this house armed with [God's] power" (D&C 109:22) and continue in faith to the end. In the temple we can come to understand we are not alone.

The sixth battle sword is *Paul.* Why should we bring *Paul* to memory as we battle with courage against the devil's wiles? Because he reminds us that we should have much hope in ourselves because the Lord has much hope in each of us. I believe the Savior went to Gethsemane and Calvary in part because he knew many, "a great multitude, which no man could number" (Revelation 7:9), would follow him through the strait gate and on the narrow way.

Saul, as he was then known, was persecuting the Church and its members, making "havock of the church" and throwing the Saints in prison (Acts 8:3). Some, like Stephen, died because of his persecution. But look what the Savior did for this enemy of the Church. He chose him for the ministry. Paul became a great Apostle, disciple, and teacher. Paul helped build the kingdom of God in a powerful and lasting way. He was persecuted, arrested, imprisoned, shipwrecked, and finally executed in Rome.

His words show us that despite his challenges he pressed forward with courage and on, on to the victory:

"We are troubled on every side, yet not distressed; we are perplexed, but not in despair; persecuted, but not forsaken; cast down, but not destroyed" (2 Corinthians 4:8–9).

"Who shall separate us from the love of Christ? shall tribulation, or distress, or persecution, or famine, or nakedness, or peril, or sword? . . . For I am persuaded, that neither death, nor life, nor angels, nor principalities, nor powers, nor things present, nor things to come, nor height, nor depth, nor any other creature, shall be able to separate us from the love of God, which is in Christ Jesus our Lord" (Romans 8:35, 38–39).

I had the opportunity to travel the same route as some of Paul's journeys and walk some of the roads he walked. While in Ephesus, our Muslim guide took us to the great theater where Paul delivered a sermon or two to the Ephesians. He explained how Paul's life was saved by his friends, how he was warned and then escaped capture from that very theater.

I was deeply touched as this guide spoke with such respect about Paul. Here was a Muslim who did not believe in any of Paul's teachings, but he respected him for his great service to Christianity. He told us that he believed that no one had worked harder than Paul to spread Christianity. He said that Paul had done more than anyone else on the earth to further Christianity in the world. He called him an "exceedingly good man and hard worker."

Paul believed in victory, no matter how long and hard the road. I traveled some of Paul's roads by automobile. He walked every mile. Those routes, roads, and distances covered by Paul are staggering. It must have been terribly difficult. It must have required tremendous sacrifice. He taught us by his hard work a great example of having courage, even when persecuted and oppressed.

I traveled with clients recently, and my courage was put to a test. Many of my clients have the luxury of traveling by private jet. Usually when we get on board, there is no socializing of any kind. We spread our plans or construction documents on a table and everyone talks about the project we are working on.

But this occasion was different. Their large plane was being serviced so we took a smaller, eight-passenger jet.

I found myself in the back of the plane; my clients, husband and wife, were seated in front of me. It was a small cabin and our knees almost touched as we faced each other. There was no way to pull out documents or discuss design details, and they seemed to want to just visit.

They asked about my family. They asked about my son on his mission. Then, out of nowhere the husband asked me, "How on earth did you get into this Mormon deal anyway?"

Normally I would take an opportunity like this to bear my testimony. But you need to know that this man can be extremely coarse and caustic at times. And he has teased me constantly about being "Mormon." He makes jokes about tithing and the time I spend at church or in Church service. Sometimes his teasing is borderline rude, and it is always judgmental.

However, I know that he respects me tremendously too. In

meetings with wealthy and powerful men, he has deferred to me and my judgment. A well-known "fortune" magazine named him one of the ten wealthiest men in the Western States. He is accustomed to hiring people he trusts and respects. Often he gives me the final decision on an issue.

The teasing perhaps is meant to be a sign of friendship, but sometimes it has been just plain ridiculous.

So at this moment I hesitated, unsure of how I should answer. Should I just give a generic response about my parents converting when I was a young child? It flashed through my mind that if I told him more I could open myself up to more teasing and caustic jabs.

Suddenly I thought of Paul and his hard work—and the intense persecution. And I thought of my missionary son, who was walking in Paul's footsteps as a missionary. Their sacrifices for the truth's sake pierced my heart, and I felt a powerful spirit envelop me.

I bore my testimony to them of how my parents had converted and how I had come to my own desire to know the truth about religion. I told them my conversion story and was able to tell them that I knew the Church was true and why. I stated that President Hinckley was the prophet and told them of my understanding of the Book of Mormon.

For twenty minutes I spoke with the power and sweetness that comes only by the Holy Ghost. I knew they felt something. They asked me to tell them of my husband's conversion story as well.

To this day, my client has not teased me anymore.

I received a letter from a sister who had experienced tremendous adversity in her life. She had seen death, lost loved ones, and been abused. Her marriage had ended in divorce. She shared heartbreaking experiences with me. As she concluded her letter, she stated, "I have scars, physical and emotional scars. I am so afraid they are there forever."

She need not wish for those scars to go. They are, in a certain sense, medals. President Hugh B. Brown once said: "At the bar the Judge will not look us over for medals, degrees, or diplomas, but for scars" ("A Time of Testing," *Improvement Era*, June 1969, p. 99).

Paul said somewhat the same: "I have fought a good fight, I have finished my course, I have kept the faith: henceforth there is laid up for me a crown of righteousness, which the Lord, the righteous judge, shall give me at that day: and not to me only, but unto all them also that love his appearing" (2 Timothy 4:7–8).

Two years before his death, Joseph Smith, a man well acquainted by this time with violence, mobs, beatings, persecution, and sorrow of every kind, wrote these glorious words:

"Now, what do we hear in the gospel which we have received? A voice of gladness! . . . glad tidings of great joy . . . giving us consolation by holding forth that which is to come, confirming our hope! Brethren, shall we not go on in so great a cause? Go forward and not backward. Courage, brethren; and on, on to the victory!" (D&C 128:19, 21–22).

Through this victory we can move on, on to the greatness that awaits us.

CHAPTER FOUR

For Such a Time As This

Who are you?

Really, who are you? Why were you born?

Will your life have mattered? What is your special mission in life, or is there one?

This is the ultimate struggle for each of us, to discover who we really are and why we were born. And then, to act like who we really are—not like what we think is popular or fashionable or clever or even what other people want us to be. Rather, we yearn to discover for ourselves that we are truly sons and daughters of God and heirs to the thrones and principalities of God. After this discovery our duty is to act like it and understand why we were born, to live the life of a Latter-day Saint *through* our path of duty.

We say, "I am a daughter of God" or "I am a son of God," but so many of us don't quite get it.

Esther got it.

Perhaps there is no greater female example of faith in individual purpose of life than the girl-queen Esther.

She enters the historical record timidly, perhaps filled with the same fears and doubts we feel, and then strides triumphantly across a few pages of the Old Testament. She fights literally for her life—and for the lives of her people. In the end she finds victory—for herself, for her people, and for her God.

Esther was married to the king. Apparently the king had no idea that she was Hebrew when he was tricked into signing a death decree for all Hebrew people. Her uncle asked her to save her people. Esther knew that to go to the king without being summoned by him could possibly mean her own immediate death. She hesitated, and then her uncle spoke, "For if thou altogether holdest thy peace at this time, then shall there enlargement and deliverance arise to the Jews from another place; . . . and who knoweth whether thou are come into the kingdom for such a time as this?" (Esther 4:14).

Esther accepted her *path of duty.*

Why is it so hard to discover for ourselves who we are, why we were born, and why we were born *now?* Perhaps the answer to that question has something to do with the family we are born into, a poor use of our agency, certain mistakes we've made, our own weaknesses, or perhaps even poor teachings in our youth. Maybe it's difficult to discover who we are because our spiritual world doesn't match the physical one we live in because we're poor, not so attractive, or perhaps not the best student.

Animals know who they are. Rabbits seem to know they're rabbits. They certainly act like rabbits. Ducks act like ducks; horses act like horses. Why do we—sons and daughters of God, heirs to thrones and principalities, potentially future gods and goddesses—have such a tough time knowing who we are so we can act like it?

Author Stephen E. Robinson has written: "Perhaps the greatest spiritual frustration many people encounter is that without exception we mortals are *converted* long before we can be *perfected.* That means all of us limp along for a considerable period of time in which our commitment and desire are not matched by our actual performance" (*Following Christ* [Salt Lake City: Deseret Book Co., 1995], p. vii).

When we were given a name and a blessing as babies or baptized at age eight, our names were recorded on the records of the Church. But more significant than that, our Father in Heaven knows who we are—and where we are—and he put us here "for such a time as this."

We must simply trust that the Savior is hard at work helping us—not in spite of the difficulties, mistakes, and weaknesses of our lives, but because of them. If we will believe him when he says he is helping us, we will better be able to keep the commandments. And keeping the commandments is what will show us who we really are.

There are a lot of commandments. Trying to keep track of all of them is like trying to keep dandelions from blowing apart in the wind. We have discussed the duty we have as Latter-day Saints to obey, repent, and forgive. But there is a commandment greater than all the rest. In fact, if we can grasp this one concept and truly strive to live it right, then we automatically live many of the other laws too.

It is the law of love.

"Master, which is the great commandment in the law? Jesus said unto him, Thou shalt love the Lord thy God. . . . And the second is like unto it, Thou shalt love thy neighbour as thyself" (Matthew 22:36–39). This is not ecclesiastical rhetoric. It is not fluffy emotional stuff. It is not a soap opera story. Nor is it a discussion that makes us look good and feel good but then is easily just forgotten.

There is a true answer here in those verses—an answer to the question, "Who are you?" You are a son or daughter of God, and the purpose of all this hard work here in this world is to make us

Christlike. If through our humble obedience we can love God and each other, we will learn to love ourselves. Through love and service to others we will discover who we really are—and then act like it.

The world would tell us that we cannot love others until we love ourselves, that we can't feel good about ourselves until we have self-esteem, and self-esteem can only come from successes. The Savior has taught us that no matter how we feel about ourselves, we are expected to make good choices. Those choices include loving others and striving to keep the commandments. No matter how we feel about ourselves, if we start serving and loving others and keeping the commandments we will feel better about ourselves. Through consistency, not perfection, we will love ourselves even enough to know who we are and why we were born—and that we were indeed born for such a time as this.

And what a time this is!

This is a time of moving the kingdom of God from a relatively small nucleus to global proportions. Do you have any doubt the Church is preparing for a larger and larger community of believers?

In the words of Joseph Smith: "The Standard of Truth has been erected; no unhallowed hand can stop the work from progressing; persecutions may rage, mobs may combine, armies may assemble, calumny may defame, but the truth of God will go forth boldly, nobly, and independent, till it has penetrated every continent, visited every clime, swept every country, and sounded in every ear, till the purposes of God shall be accomplished, and the Great Jehovah shall say the work is done" (*The Teachings of Joseph Smith*, ed. Larry E. Dahl and Donald Q. Cannon [Salt Lake City: Bookcraft, 1997], pp. 684–85).

It's going to take a people who really know who they are to see this great unfolding through.

As we see the borders of the Church expand and a global

surge of membership begin to unfold, we can be certain we will have the opportunity to live and work among many who will be quite different from us. They will come into our midst from different lifestyles, different cultures, different levels of understanding. Some may even be in our own family! This is great! We have a wonderful opportunity to be "an example of the believers" and act like who we are (1 Timothy 4:12).

Paul had an understanding of this very issue when he wrote to the Corinthians and compared the value of every member of the Church to the parts of the body. He taught us that every member matters, and the weakest member matters most of all.

"For the body is not one member, but many. If the foot shall say, Because I am not the hand, I am not part of the body; is it therefore not of the body? And if the ear shall say, Because I am not the eye, I am not of the body; it is therefore not of the body? If the whole body were an eye, where were the hearing? . . . And if they were all one member, where were the body? But now are they many members, yet but one body. And the eye cannot say unto the hand, I have no need of thee: nor again the head to the feet, I have no need of you. Nay, much more those members of the body, which seem to be more feeble, are necessary. . . . That there should be no schism in the body; but that the members should have the same care one for another. And whether one member suffer, all the members suffer with it; or one member be honoured, all the members rejoice with it. Now ye are the body of Christ, and members in particular" (1 Corinthians 12:14–17, 19–22, 25–27).

Animals know who they are, and they act like it. We, the community of believers, the covenanted people, have to know who we are and then act like it. Then the Lord will be able to use us and raise us up to nobility so that our talents will help prepare the kingdom for such a time as this.

There is an age-old truth that if you desire to possess a certain quality, that quality can be developed by acting as if you already possess it. If we want to know who we are, we must act like believers.

"Be thou an example of the believers, in word, in conversation, in charity, in spirit, in faith, in purity. Till I come, give attendance to reading, to exhortation, to doctrine. Neglect not the gift that is in thee, which was given thee by prophecy, with the laying on of the hands of the presbytery. Meditate upon these things; give thyself wholly to them; that thy profiting may appear to all. Take heed unto thyself, and unto the doctrine; continue in them: for in doing this thou shalt both save thyself, and them that hear thee" (Timothy 4:12–16).

Be Thou an Example of the Believers in Word and Conversation

We can improve our language. We can be more careful of the words we use. We can strive for better grammar, less crude and vulgar words, and more interesting speech.

But perhaps even more pressing is our need as individuals and as a people to be exceedingly careful to not backbite, gossip, or judge one another. And there is another growing concern: murmuring among members and criticism of our Church leaders on any level.

When we allow these words and expressions into our conversations, it becomes obvious that we don't know who we are. Are we disciples, or merely members?

"Therefore thou art inexcusable, O man, whosoever thou art that judgest: for wherein thou judgest another, thou condemnest thyself; for thou that judgest doest the same thing" (Romans 2:1). In other words, when we judge another, we are really revealing our own motives. As examples of the believers and disciples who are helping prepare the world for the Second Coming, our words and conversations must be uplifting. We also need to be examples by not even listening to those who defame and downgrade others.

I have a friend who will inspire you when I tell you what she did for me. She didn't tell me what happened, but someone else present that day told me of how my friend Devra was an example of the believers.

There were a number of women gathered together for some occasion, when the conversation turned to gossip laced with criticism. The person they began to discuss was me. My friend Devra listened for a few minutes, then stood up and quietly said, "That's my friend you're talking about, and I need to leave now." Then she left.

She didn't condemn; she led by example. My friend Devra knows who she is. At that moment, with those women, she had come into the kingdom for such a time as this.

Others watch us, especially those not of our faith. We have a duty to be examples in our words and conversations. If we are not careful, our words will condemn us.

We also must be examples in word and conversation as regards our Church leaders. When we criticize our Church leaders, we criticize the Savior's work. The programs of the Church aren't always designed to find the perfect person for the calling; sometimes is is a matter of finding the person who can be better perfected through the calling. The Church is a brilliant organization, designed to help the weakest Saint among us. As Paul pointed out in his letter to the Corinthians, every member matters and the weakest member matters most of all!

Part of working with one another is increasing our love, charity, and patience, not in spite of one another's weaknesses but because of them. What an unbelievable opportunity to become more and more Christlike!

If we murmur about or criticize our leaders we could easily find ourselves joined among those at Capernaum who, having been personally instructed by Jesus, began to murmur: "Many therefore of his disciples, when they had heard this, said, This is an hard saying; who can hear it? When Jesus knew in himself that his disciples murmured at it, he said unto them, Doth this offend you? . . . From that time many of his disciples went back, and walked no more with him" (John 6:60–61, 66).

Our admonition is instead to follow Peter's example of a true believer: "Then said Jesus unto the twelve, Will ye also go away? Then Simon Peter answered him, Lord, to whom shall we go? thou hast the words of eternal life. And we believe and are sure that thou are that Christ, the Son of the living God" (John 6:67–69). Peter knew the Savior had come into the kingdom for such a time as this.

Be Thou an Example of the Believers in Charity

Charity is just not that easy. Brotherly kindness is very easy. It's easy to love and serve people who respond positively and are loving people in themselves. But charity is a bit of a stretch for most of us. Let's look at a description of what it is: "And charity suffereth long, and is kind, and envieth not, and is not puffed up, seeketh not her own, is not easily provoked, thinketh no evil, and rejoiceth not in iniquity but rejoiceth in the truth, beareth all things, believeth all things, hopeth all things, endureth all things" (Mormon 7:45).

And again in the next verse, it becomes clear that unless we have charity we won't know who we are: "Wherefore, my beloved brethren, if ye have not charity, ye are nothing, for charity never faileth. Wherefore, cleave unto charity, which is the greatest of all" (verse 46).

Charity will not fail us; indeed, charity helps us know who we are: "Pray unto the Father with all the energy of heart, that ye may be filled with this love, which he hath bestowed upon all who are true followers of his Son, Jesus Christ, . . . that when he shall appear we shall be like him" (Moroni 7:48).

A good brother took his ten-year-old son to lunch at one of those self-service salad bar restaurants. Loitering in front of the restaurant was a disheveled and very dirty vagrant who held a sign asking for money. This father decided it would be an excellent teaching moment for his son on the principle of charity, so he reached into his pocket and gave the man a dollar.

Later, after they were seated, he was able to observe that most of the entering patrons rebuffed or ignored the beggar. He felt very good that he had extended a helping hand towards someone so repulsive and had been able to demonstrate this nonjudgment to his son.

He later said that he felt good, perhaps even smug, until he saw another man, a member of his ward, stop and begin to converse with the vagrant. They seemed to strike up a very friendly conversation, and his fellow ward member appeared to be enjoying the visit.

Then, my friend witnessed an act not unlike something the Master himself might have done. He saw this priesthood leader open the door and usher the beggar in. He watched him pay for his meal, eat lunch with him, and intensely involve himself in genuine dialogue with him; and as they stood up to leave, he watched this example of one of the believers put some money in the palm of "one of the least of these," our brethren (see Matthew 25:31–45).

We can all do better can't we?

One of the most unforgettable people I have ever met was a

man named Jim. When I met him he was a young married husband fresh out of BYU and newly settled in his first teaching position in a local school in Las Vegas.

He and his wife had a small baby, rented a very humble house, and didn't have much money. But he was a true follower, a true believer.

He was called to be the deacons quorum adviser. In this quorum were about a dozen boys; however, at the time of his call only five or six were active. He was told that it had been difficult to get the other boys to come because there were many other distractions, such as sports, paper routes, and lack of family support.

But Jim believed the Savior would want them all there, all of them. So he began to seek guidance.

One day an idea came to him. He had earned his way through college by fixing and selling old cars. If he bought an old car and parked it in his backyard, he could have the boys come every Saturday. Through working on the car together they would build camaraderie, love, and brotherhood. To make it appealing, he would tell them that when the car was sold, they would use the money to go to Disneyland. (This was before the advent of the budget allowance program.)

It must have been a sacrifice for this young couple to come up with the front money for the car and the replacement parts. And it was perhaps an even greater sacrifice to designate every Saturday to this project.

He recruited the active deacons to help him invite the less-active ones. He made personal visits to their homes; he made many phone calls.

Every Saturday he was in the driveway, waiting for the boys. Some Saturdays many showed up, some Saturdays only one, and some Saturdays none. But little by little, week after week, month after month the boys began to respond. The less-active boys began to attend church. It was sporadic at first, but camaraderie around that old car began to turn into friendship. As the months rolled on, friendship became brotherhood and brotherhood turned into love. There was a very special spirit in that quorum.

All but one boy became completely active. The lone deacon who had never come out, even once, had no interest in the Church, and neither did his family.

The car was finished. It was sold for a good profit, and they were all excited to go to Disneyland.

Jim was concerned about this lone deacon who had never participated. He phoned him and invited him on the trip anyway. The boy wasn't interested and hung up on him.

The trip to Disneyland was exhausting, but the bonding between them all was deepened. They were united; they were one.

Nevertheless, one was missing, and Jim couldn't rest. His love had grown so much for his young friends that he wanted the lost boy to be brought home to the fold.

That next day he called the boy and reminded him who he was, his deacons quorum adviser. And then he added, "I want you to be a part of the quorum. We need you there. You are missed. Sunday I am going to pick you up for church."

The boy immediately became irritated and told Jim he was not going to come to church, so he shouldn't bother to come by. Jim responded, "I am coming to pick you up. I'll be there on time."

That Sunday he drove to the boy's home, parked in front of the house, walked to the door, and rang the bell. He waited . . . and waited. Then he rang the bell again. The door opened and a sleepy twelve-year-old, pajama-clad boy stood looking in disbelief.

"I told you I wasn't coming to church!"

Jim answered firmly but warmly, "I came to pick you up and I'm not leaving until you come with me."

"Then you can sit out there in your car all day," the boy said as he shut the door.

So Jim went back to his car and waited. Very soon he saw the curtains moving. Then more minutes passed and they moved again. After about twenty minutes the door opened and the pajama-clad boy stomped down the sidewalk. He opened the car door and asked, "You aren't going to leave, are you?" and Jim said, "Yes, when you come with me—and next Sunday I'll be back again."

The deacon became quiet and then thoughtfully stated, "Okay. I'll come this one Sunday if you won't come back again." Jim said, "Well, hurry and get ready, and we'll only miss the opening song."

The boy emerged ten minutes later, buttons on his shirt undone, shoes and socks in hand, hair tousled, and not too happy about the whole affair. But he got in the car and they drove to the meetinghouse.

With all the love and brotherhood already in the quorum because of their experiences together, their class had a special spirit, a spirit that enveloped the lost deacon. They welcomed him with open arms and unusual enthusiasm for twelve-year-olds. Perhaps they radiated the love of Jim for all of them.

On the way home Jim said, "I'll pick you up same time next Sunday."

"Wait a minute! I thought we had an agreement—I'd come today and you would leave me alone."

"I never agreed to that. I just told you to go get dressed," Jim said. And then he added, "It wasn't so bad, was it? In fact, couldn't you see how glad everyone was to see you, how much we want you there? Please, please come back next Sunday."

The boy looked at his dirty tennis shoes and stared a long while. The spirit of love must have touched him deeply in those few hours among the believers. He said, "Well, it wasn't *that* bad. I guess I could come back one more time."

The next Sunday, Jim arrived as scheduled. He had to knock on the door, then wait while the young man got ready and walked down to the car, shirt unbuttoned, shoes in hand, hair tousled.

But again, charity, the pure love of Christ, must have touched his heart, because he agreed to return the next Sunday too.

The same scene was repeated Sunday after Sunday until the "one more time" turned into weeks without missing. Jim was filled with love and dedication to this small member of the Savior's flock.

Can you imagine his joy when one Sunday as he lifted his hand to knock on the door, it suddenly opened and there stood his deacon, shirt buttoned, shoes on, hair combed, tie in hand!

This scene was repeated week after week until now, many months later, Jim rounded the corner and could not contain his tears as he saw his little friend standing on the curb, dressed and ready to go to church with him.

Jim knew the greatest difficulty in his calling would be losing this deacon to the teachers quorum; even though he was so instrumental in preparing them for advancement, he missed each one. His special deacon was now at the end of his second year and nearing advancement. Jim had picked him up every Sunday for nearly two years or had made sure someone had taken him. He looked forward to those visits in the car, for they had had some very spiritual talks.

So you can imagine his dismay when one Sunday as he rounded the corner, his deacon wasn't there. Right away he feared something was wrong. The boy had never failed to call him if he couldn't make it or was ill. They were true friends. What had happened?

He darted up the sidewalk and rang the bell. What a surprise when the door opened and he saw the boy all dressed and ready to go!

"Oh, Brother Jones, I am so sorry! I forgot to call you. I was so excited I just forgot to call you. Brother Jones, I won't be needing a ride this morning! This morning, *I'm taking my dad!*"

Because of Jim's example of the pure love of Christ, an entire family was reactivated and later sealed in the temple as a family. Jim knew not only who he was but also who his deacons were—all of them. Is there any doubt Jim had come into the kingdom for such a time as this?

Be Thou an Example of the Believers in Spirit

What kind of a spirit comes from our countenances? I love the ancient proverb that goes like this: "The best mirror you will ever have is the face of a friend."

If the Savior is your friend, you will better grasp the scripture, "Have ye received his image in your countenances?" (Alma 5:14).

If we know who we are, when dark clouds of trouble hang over us our spirit will radiate the image of peace and power, the image of the Savior. We will show outwardly our faith and hope in the knowledge that a plan for each of us is unfolding and the Savior is directing the work here on earth.

Does the spirit we carry and radiate provide strong witness to others that we do indeed know who we are and that our spirituality is proof that God is in our lives and that we glorify him by showing how much he has done for us?

Brother Clark is an example of the believers in spirit. He lives in the Hawaiian islands. When my daughter was on her mission there, she and her companion would see him many times on the Kahuku Highway. They knew as they waved and honked at him that he was either on his way to do his home teaching or to do someone else's home teaching who couldn't or wouldn't do it, or he was going to visit a less-active member.

He was incredibly diligent in doing this, even in the rain, and it rains a lot in Hawaii. Once in a while the rain did interfere with his three-mile visits, but only because Brother Clark traveled the Kahuku Highway in his electric wheelchair.

As a young man he was paralyzed from the neck down and has spent his adult life bound to his wheelchair, dependent on others to physically care for him. He has served in many Church callings and leadership positions. He is a man who understands his stewardship to "do unto others" because Brother Clark knows who he is.

There have undoubtedly been some dark hours in his life for he is a man who suffers physical pain. But those who know him are unaware of this because Brother Clark is of good cheer and constantly looks to do good works and glorify his Father in Heaven.

Brother Clark travels this highway in his wheelchair to lift the spirits of his widowed friends, the sick in body or heart, the lonely, the forgotten. Never a murmuring word escapes his tongue; rather, he is always grateful for a chance to serve and radiates gratitude for his many blessings.

Brother Clark knows who he is. He has through his common lot come into the kingdom for such a time as this!

Be Thou an Example of the Believers in Faith

What legacy will we leave to our posterity? There is absolute certainty that in a coming day each of us will face another great difficulty. Will we demonstrate to our children and our children's children that we believe what we have always taught them? Will we show them that we know who we are? Will they talk about our faith in a treasured story that will be passed on through generations yet to come and perhaps through all eternity? Not sensational stories, but "common lot" stories of our tried and true testimonies developed through our trust and faith in the Lord.

When my father was president of a little New England branch, he met two outstanding examples of believers in an elderly and infirm homebound couple who were struggling to exist on social security.

One Saturday he was working on his car when the impression came to him to go and visit this couple. Now, you have to understand, the branch stretched for over seventy-five miles in each direction. He always took them the sacrament each Sunday and so dismissed the impression with thoughts that he would visit them tomorrow anyway.

As the day wore on, the feeling that he should visit them grew stronger, until he finally quit his work and drove the seventy-five miles to their humble little home. It was dusk as he knocked on the front door. He could hear the effort it was taking for someone to answer the door. He knew that they had not been expecting him. They had no telephone, so he had been unable to tell them he was coming. He was prepared for the dimly lit room; they hardly had enough to live on, and conserving electricity was a priority. He was prepared for the smell of medicine and closed quarters—they were feeble and not well.

But he was not prepared for the greeting he received as they opened the door!

"Oh, Brother Rodriguez, come in; we've been expecting you! We have been praying all day that you would come. We have something to give you."

Even in the dimly lit room he could see what the husband clutched in his hand—an envelope, and on it in shaky script was the word *tithing*.

They then proceeded to tell my father that every Sunday they took the sacrament, but they hadn't paid tithing in a long time. They loved the Savior, they were certain of his love for them, and his sacrifice meant everything to them. They wanted to pay their tithing and they wanted to pay it that day, before they took the sacrament again.

At first my father wanted to refuse. He knew of their dire circumstances. But he listened to their sweet and pure words. When the sixty-one dollars and ten cents were placed in his hand, he had to restrain the tears as the couple said, "This is a full tithe."

Sixty-one dollars was a large amount of money to their meager existence, but he felt the Spirit inspire him to accept it.

He left their home. Stirred by their faith, he didn't want to drive home without offering a prayer asking the Lord to bless them.

He walked out on to their property and knelt in a secluded area near an old building in the back. The sun was starting to fade and the hour was peaceful. As he meditated on what their needs really were and what he wanted to say in his prayer, he suddenly became aware of the small bushes all around him that seemed to have a strange dark berry on them.

He got closer and began to examine them—they were blueberries! However, they were black and hard and the bushes were not doing well. He surveyed the area. There were acres and acres of blueberry bushes. The shed had equipment for harvesting, even cartons of boxes and supplies. All of a sudden an idea came!

The branch could harvest the blueberries. Delicious, expensive blueberries would bring this faithful couple enough money to make it through the winter.

Almost as suddenly as the idea came he realized why the farm was inactive and the bushes looked so unhealthy. New England was having the worst drought in forty years.

He knelt down and prayed simply, "Father, these two old people have enough faith to pay their tithing; will you please send the rain?" and then he explained his plans and opened a fast.

Day after day he checked the forecast. Hot summer days, no relief in sight. He kept on praying. On the fifth morning he woke up and heard the rain on the roof. He turned on the news immediately. A mid-Atlantic storm had suddenly changed course in the middle of the night and headed for the New England states. It rained for weeks. Just enough rain, too. The blueberries got big and fat and expensive. The branch harvested and helped distribute the blueberries. The couple received enough money to live comfortably through the winter. Many in the branch who had been reluctant to pay their tithing began to have enough faith to do so, and testimonies increased.

This couple were examples to many and had indeed come into the kingdom for such a time as this. This couple knew who they were.

Be Thou an Example of
the Believers in Purity

"Blessed are the pure in heart" (Matthew 5:8).

I met a woman in Oregon named Linda, a sister in the gospel who has been an example of the believers in purity.

One night the phone rang, and her young daughter answered it. "Mommy, it's for you. It's an old friend."

The voice on the other end of the line was a man. He asked if she was the same Linda (and he repeated her maiden name) from such and such a town. When she answered that she was, he introduced himself as a friend from the past. She remembered him right away. They had dated a little when she was in high school. He had wanted the relationship to be more, but she had just been his friend. He wasn't a member of the Church, and she had lost track of him after high school.

She listened as he began to explain why he was calling: "Linda, I have been searching for you for one year."

He then told her that he was now a member of the Church; in fact, he was a bishop and had a young family. About a year prior to this they had held a special family home evening on missionary work. They had invited the full-time missionaries and some converts into their home to teach their children a few principles. The converts had been invited to talk about the missionaries who had brought them the gospel and what the missionaries' sacrifice had meant to each of them.

During the lesson, one of his children said, "Dad, you are a convert. Who was your missionary?" This father then told them about his conversion.

As he thought about this evening in the days that followed, he remembered Linda's influence in his life. She was pure in body and mind and heart. This had attracted him because he could feel her wholesomeness and her inner strength. He told her that he had watched her carefully during their high school years. Her example to him had helped him many times when he himself felt weak. He said that when he was in college, he noticed some people that had the same countenance of purity as Linda. It was a tremendous contrast to the "party people" he observed.

He sought these individuals out and learned that they too were Latter-day Saints. He became involved with them, was eventually baptized, and even went on a mission. Now he was married in the temple and active in the gospel.

He concluded by saying: "I had to find you, Linda. I had to

tell you that *you* were my missionary. Your purity, your example never left me, and it inspired me and led me to find what it was that made you that way."

He recognized that Linda knew who she was and she had acted like it. So powerful was her example of the believers that an entire new lineage had come forth because of her influence in his life. Linda had come into the kingdom for such a time as this.

In the letter, quoted earlier, in which he exhorted Timothy to be "an example of the believers," the Apostle Paul went on to admonish him and, by extension, all of us to read the scriptures, bear our testimonies, and follow the doctrine of the gospel and counsel of the prophets. And we are to continue in these things, or, in other words, we must endure to the end (see 1 Timothy 4:13–16).

My friend Rachel is a grandmother and great-grandmother.

She was born on a sheep ranch in Wyoming. Her father was a wealthy, successful rancher and had thousands of head of sheep.

When Rachel was five years old, she became desperately ill. The doctor came to see her several times. There were no hospitals in their part of the country in those early decades of the twentieth century.

Rachel's conditions worsened. One night the doctor solemnly told the family that she would probably die during the night. He had done all he could do, and now it was just too late.

Rachel had been the last child, the light and heart of her devoted father. He was overcome with grief. He put on his hat and coat and rode out on his horse to some secluded corner of his ranch. There he knelt in the dirt and wept and pleaded for the life of his beautiful daughter.

With hat in hand, he humbly bowed before the Lord and offered his own life in exchange for hers. He was willing to pay whatever price the Lord would extract from him.

I do not know how long he prayed, how long he was gone. But his petition was intense and earnest and desperate. He came forth from the prayer with a calmness and an assurance that Rachel's life would be spared, but a price would be paid.

Within days Rachel was strengthened. By the end of the week she was actually running around the yard as if nothing had ever been wrong. The family offered a fast of thanksgiving.

A few weeks later, the price of the miracle was exacted. A range fire swept across the thousands of acres of her father's ranch and destroyed all of the land and all of the sheep. He was left destitute and never recovered financially.

Over the years, he told this story to Rachel. He reiterated time and again how valuable she was, how important her life's work was, and how gladly he would pay that price again.

She grew up wondering what her special mission in life was to be. She went to college, got married in the temple, raised a large family, held numerous Church positions, and supported her husband in his leadership callings. She never had a career, never received much notice for any talent she possessed, made bread and rolls about as well as anyone else, and never had her name in the newspaper.

Throughout the first part of her life she wondered continually for what special purpose the Lord had preserved her at so great a cost to her father and family. Why was she born?

When she was in her fifties and her life had been filled with the common lot ordinary work of mankind, she learned one day the Hebrew meaning of her name *Rachel*. It means ewe, young lamb, or little lamb.

Suddenly she understood! Her father had sacrificed little lambs for the one lamb of greatest value to him and to his posterity throughout both time and eternity. Her great mission was to do the common lot ordinary work of mankind. She had been saved to stand as a witness of God's hand in our lives, his love for families, his continuation of the seeds of life, his compassion and his desire to see us return home. Rachel realized she had come into the kingdom for such a time as this.

Do you doubt who you are?

Is there any question of the greatness of your lives?

"My name is Jehovah, and I know the end from the beginning; therefore my hand shall be over thee. And I will make of thee a great nation, and I will bless thee above measure, . . . for as many as receive this Gospel shall be called after thy name. . . . I give unto thee a promise that this right shall continue in thee, and in thy seed after thee . . . shall all the families of the earth be blessed, even with the blessings of the Gospel, which are the blessings of salvation, even of life eternal" (Abraham 2:8–11).

Is there any doubt why we were born?

The conclusion becomes inescapable; as with Esther our sister, we have been born to bless the lives of others with our spiritual gifts and indeed have come into the kingdom at a specific time and place, for such a time as this.

CHAPTER FIVE

Learn of Him

We can almost hear the voices of prophets speaking, pleading, across the centuries through the pages of all the scriptures, "Keep the commandments; keep the commandments! In this there is safety; in this there is peace" (*Hymns*, no. 303).

As mentioned previously, President Heber J. Grant instructed us that "living the life of a Latter-day Saint," or simply following a *path of duty*, is what will ultimately save us. "Keep the commandments" is the direction from the Savior. "Canst thou be humble and meek, and conduct thyself wisely before me? Yea, come unto me thy Savior" (D&C 19:41).

In the Doctrine and Covenants we find instruction to Church members regarding their duty after they are baptized. We are to have "a godly walk and conversation" and have "works and faith agreeable to the holy scriptures—walking in holiness before the Lord" (D&C 20:69). Then comes the admonition to "meet together often to partake of bread and wine in the remembrance of the Lord Jesus" so that we may "always remember him and keep his commandments" (D&C 20:75, 77).

The Savior has invited us to remember him always so that we will think about him, his actions and example, his love for us, and his promises to us. And all of this because "as [a man] thinketh in his heart, so is he" (Proverbs 23:7).

If we think about the Savior and remember him, our hearts will change. If our hearts are changed, our behavior will come closer and closer to being Christlike. We need to always remember him so that we won't forget how to be like him.

If our hearts are changed we can become humble and meek and conduct ourselves wisely before the Lord. It will take a humble and meek person to follow a simple path of duty, to live the life of a Latter-day Saint.

One day, across the centuries of this mortal sphere, there will rise such "a great multitude . . . of all nations, and kindreds, and people, and tongues" who will stand before the throne of the Savior "clothed with white robes and palms in their hands" (Revelation 7:9). These are great men and great women who have come "out of great tribulation" (Revelation 7:14), kept the commandments and remembered the Savior always, and have tried by simple duty to do what is right.

We remember the Savior and discover our own greatness by developing generosity and then striving to be more and more generous.

Latter-day Saint generosity can readily be understood by observing our tithes and offerings and the "meals on wheels" so abundant in our church. These are not only important as regards our attitudes of generosity but also essential if we are ever to learn the principle itself. But if I want to be more and more like the Savior, then I must learn to be a generous person and not just a person who is generous in a few select areas. But just what does that mean?

I recently saw a magazine article entitled "Road Rage." It chronicled the incidents in recent years that show a growing tendency among motorists to become so angry when confronted with inconsiderate or offensive drivers that they lose all control. In these moments of utter rage, such individuals pursue the offender with extreme vengeance, which often results in property damage, bodily harm, and sometimes even death.

The article gave complex answers for why the behavior is on the rise. But is seems very simple to me: the tremendous lack of generosity among the children of men has caused "the love of many [to] wax cold" (Matthew 24:12).

A generous person never withholds sincere love. The Savior, our Perfect Exemplar, did not withhold his love even when he was being personally assaulted. The night his enemies came to get him, they found him in what they thought was a garden. We now know that place called Gethsemane to be, in a manner of speaking, a sacred, holy altar. They came to take Jesus of Nazareth, and they came to put him to death. He knew that. Here he stood—the greatest of us all. He was full of sorrow and heaviness. These had been excruciating hours of exhausting suffering and pain that none of us can comprehend, for they included even the "pains and sickness" of every man, woman, and child (Alma 7:11). A person so stricken with such suffering might understandably be unable to find generosity in such a circumstance. There would understandably be no time to think of others, especially forgive others, when every breath was labored. Yet perfect Jesus, meek and generous Jesus, restored the severed ear to the hostile soldier. The Savior denied himself any wrong reaction and lost himself in love and generosity to all mankind.

In a world growing colder because the love for others has waxed cold, there is cause to "always remember him." We are even admonished to "pray unto the Father with all the energy of heart, that ye may be filled with this love, . . . that when he shall appear we shall be like him" (Moroni 7:48).

"Then said Jesus unto his disciples, If any man will come after me, *let him deny himself*, and take up his cross, and follow me. For whosoever will save his life shall lose it: and whosoever will lose his life for my sake shall find it" (Matthew 16:24–25; emphasis added). To *deny oneself* means to sacrifice.

The Joseph Smith Translation continues this passage with a special emphasis: "And now for a man to take up his cross, is to deny himself all ungodliness, and every worldly lust, and keep my commandments" (JST, Matthew 16:26).

In other words, the "giving away" or the sacrifice by denying ourselves our sins of pride and selfishness is a requirement to become like the Savior, to become great men and great women. Without this denial too many of us will continue to indulge ourselves in our appetites, passions, opinions, and attitudes outside the Lord's boundaries.

Generosity increases as we deny ourselves wrong attitudes, feelings, and possessions. Sacrifice brings forth the blessings of heaven.

Denying oneself includes always remembering him by asking, "What would the Savior do at this moment, in this situation, in this difficulty, in this tragedy? How can I be like him here and now? What would he have me do? What is my part? How can I be more generous here and now?" Denying oneself means adopting patience and humility—on a freeway, in a crowd, with a rude clerk, with an angry or out-of-sorts loved one, even with those who have despitefully used us or born false witness against us or been offensive in any other way. Denying ourselves in these moments means we are being generous.

It has been said that "the withholding of love is the negation of the spirit of Christ, the proof that we never knew him, that for us he lived in vain" (unidentified author, quoted by Marion D. Hanks, "Forgiveness: The Ultimate Form of Love," *Ensign*, Jan. 1974, p. 20).

Withholding your love from others is a sin. Withholding love buys a ticket straight to the Theatre of Selfishness. It is perhaps one of the most insidious tools that Satan uses on basically good people. Think of the children who are unwilling to show generosity to those who love and serve them. Think of the forgotten in nursing homes. Think of the quiet, unsung acts of service rendered in the course of Sunday meetings that go unappreciated. Think now, for a moment, of the many times you have withheld a compliment or expression of love, comfort, or gratitude simply because you were in a hurry, too lazy, too fearful, or perhaps even a little jealous and resentful. Maybe you thought your remarks wouldn't matter.

Maybe it was a musical number in sacrament meeting that touched you. Perhaps a talk given by one of the youth. Maybe you are aware of someone's difficulties. Maybe your spouse gave a talk or bore his or her testimony. Maybe your husband or wife looked especially handsome or lovely one day; maybe he or she looks pretty good to you many days. Maybe a child did a chore without being told or did it with extra effort. Perhaps no one complained tonight about being summoned for family prayer. Maybe you observed a coworker being patient in a stressful moment. Maybe a waitress, clerk, or security guard displays friendliness and seems to really enjoy serving you.

There are so many opportunities in any given day to express words of love, comfort, and gratitude to lift others. Generosity is much more than money and goods and casseroles. It involves looking for ways to build and raise others. It is "losing ourselves" for the Savior's sake, and then finding ourselves, or rather the greatness in ourselves. It is truly remembering him.

Do we think all this doesn't matter? A few months ago one of our daughters sang in sacrament service. She has in recent years experienced struggles from concerns about being adopted. We hold on to her spiritually and emotionally with a tremendous outpouring of conviction and love, and she has clung to us with simple hope and a desire to feel the peace. She has emerged from the wilderness with many answers and with the peace she sought.

She possesses a beautiful voice, and music has been an important and powerful expression in her own life. She has been uplifted, sustained, and comforted with encouraging lyrics and soothing melodies.

This particular Sabbath she chose a difficult but especially moving song about the Savior. She wanted to sing her testimony. She practiced until she could perform perfectly, her voice golden as it resonated each glorious note.

That Sunday she was nervous, extremely nervous. She attends an academy for performing arts and is used to singing in public. But this occasion was different. She wanted this song to be her testimony, and she also wondered if the congregation would understand and accept her and her offering.

She sang from her heart. The Spirit filled the room. Many wiped tears from their cheeks. And her testimony was evident.

Many ward members found their way to her, sought her out, and expressed love and gratitude. Did it matter? They will never know how they lifted and raised another that day.

But being generous really isn't for others as much as it is for ourselves. How remarkable that though we deny ourselves our fears, our laziness, our apathy, and our pride, we gain greatness.

I am speaking from experience, not philosophy. I wish I could report to you that all of my experiences have been righteous. But I have in my life been ungenerous many times. I have snapped back at rude clerks, been extremely irate with disobedient children, harshly criticized another's choices, judged someone's life, passed on negative information, and withheld love and praise from someone who deserved it.

I wish I could report that all members of my immediate family are fully generous. At times they forget their blessings or get impatient with one another, and sometimes they withhold love.

I wish I could report to you that all the members of my extended family are full of generosity. In fact, many are very ungenerous. Some judge condescendingly, hold grudges, are easily offended, criticize, and withhold love and praise when it could really lift a discouraged family member.

But through the gift of the Holy Ghost, year after year, moment after moment, I am prompted to *always remember him*. We have the great blessing of the Atonement, and the power of repentance is real. As we sincerely plead for forgiveness, we feel the hope of renewed commitment. We are all improving. The Spirit helps us remember the next time we are tempted to choose foolishly so we can control our attitudes and our very words. We learn through experience after experience to remember to try to emulate the Savior in all of our actions and choices. The Holy Ghost will remind us that we especially need to be more generous. That generosity will enable us to be of one heart and one mind with the Savior. The Holy Ghost reminds us that this is part of our common lot work of mankind.

I look forward to the day when, after a lifetime of asking the question, "What would the Savior do here and now in this situation?" I won't need to ask the question any longer. I pray for the time when naturally, by my divine nature, I will automatically respond as he would. I will then have become like him.

Another way that we may always remember the Savior is by seeking the Spirit.

Seeking the Spirit means that we are responsible to pursue, petition, and cultivate the Holy Ghost into our daily lives.

A devoted grandfather wrote his posterity a final Christmas letter in December 1985. His words were brief but loving as he wrote of each one's responsibility to work hard, forgive quickly, and render service.

He concluded with this tender last message: "Remember, as

you live each day, if you lose your money, you have lost nothing. If you lose your health, you have lost something. But if you lose the Spirit, you have lost everything."

Elder Neal A. Maxwell writes: "John Donne observed that 'the memory is oftener the Holy Ghost's pulpit that he preaches in.' . . . Memory digests and assimilates the blessings we receive from God. On one occasion, Jesus observed of His disciples that they did 'not understand'; furthermore, they did 'neither remember' (see Matthew 16:8–10). Remembering and understanding should be daily conceptual companions. We need the Spirit daily to help us remember daily. Otherwise memory lapses will occur when we are most vulnerable. It is not natural to the natural man to remember yesterday's blessings gratefully, especially when today's needs of the flesh press steadily upon him. The Spirit also brings us increased understanding as it teaches us" (*Lord, Increase Our Faith* [Salt Lake City: Bookcraft, 1994], p. 102).

The Holy Ghost will inspire us to greatness. He will *never* inspire us to despair, to mediocrity, to lies of any kind.

"Behold, my brethren, he that prophesieth, let him prophesy to the understanding of men; for the Spirit speaketh the truth and lieth not. Wherefore, it speaketh of things as they really are, and of things as they really will be; wherefore, these things are manifested unto us plainly, for the salvation of our souls. But behold, we are not witnesses alone in these things; for God also spake them unto prophets of old" (Jacob 4:13).

The Holy Ghost speaks the truth and does not lie. If the Holy Ghost shows us our weaknesses, he does so that we may improve, not despair. One of his main missions is to inspire us to greatness. When Satan shows us our weaknesses, he does so to crush us, to tempt us to discouragement and despair, to cause us to forget who we really are and what we really are meant to be. The Holy Ghost, on the other hand, shows us things as they really are—yes, I need to be more generous; I need to stop criti-cizing; I need to praise others more; I need to improve here or there. He shows us what we can do to improve. I can write thank-you notes to those who touch me, I can speak compli-ments, I can stop looking for the bad in others, I can look for the good. I know from experience that he will show us "things as they really are." I know the Lord loves me to show me these weaknesses. He truly is helping me to improve, to walk the walk and not just talk the talk. I feel my Savior's love. I can be like him. I *will* be like him.

If we honor our commitments as the covenant people of the Lord Jesus Christ, we are born of the water and of the Spirit. Anyone who is born of the Spirit will be led to the temple. The Holy Ghost will always lead people to the temple.

President J Ballard Washburn, president of the Las Vegas Temple, recently spoke in my stake conference. He gave counsel to both the temple recommend holders and those who currently have no recommend and have never had one. I was so touched and impressed by his words.

Surely these sacred temples provide a place for remembering. We remember our forefathers, our progenitors, and we remember their worth. We remember the Lord our God, and there is noth-ing so symbolic on the earth in remembering the Savior as in our temples.

In the temple we turn our hearts to the fathers; there we also turn our hearts to our children and to our posterity yet to come. The protection needed to save our children and our posterity, not just in this life but throughout all eternity, if found in the temple. In this holy house we can come to know, really know, that we are of great worth, great men and great women, and we too are remembered.

The Holy Ghost will teach everyone of us on our own level.

The temple is the Lord's university where, through personal revelation and words of instruction the word of God will come into our minds. We will receive protection against the devil in his effort to destroy families.

"Holy Father, we ask thee to assist us, thy people, . . . that all people who shall enter upon the threshold of the Lord's house may feel thy power, and feel constrained to acknowledge that thou hast sanctified it, and that it is thy house, a place of thy holiness. And do thou grant, Holy Father, that all those who shall worship in this house may be taught words of wisdom . . . and that they may seek learning even by study, and also by faith, . . . and receive a fulness of the Holy Ghost. . . . And we ask thee, Holy Father, that thy servants may go forth from this house armed with thy power, and that thy name may be upon them, and thy glory be round about them, and thine angels have charge over them. . . . Remember all thy church, O Lord, with all their families, and all their immediate connections, with all their sick and afflicted ones, with all the poor and meek of the earth; that the kingdom, which thou hast set up without hands, may become a great mountain and fill the whole earth; . . . that our garments may be pure, that we may be clothed upon with robes of righteousness, with palms in our hands, and crowns of glory upon our heads, and reap eternal joy for all our sufferings" (D&C 109:10, 13–15, 22, 72, 76).

The words of this dedicatory prayer of the Kirtland Temple declare that from our temples we can "go forth" and be "armed with . . . power," even the Lord's power, and "angels will have charge" over us.

President Washburn said that yes, we go to the temple to redeem the dead, and to renew our covenants, and to feel peace, and to give service. But he instructed our stake clearly that the number one reason for going to the temple is to call down the powers and blessings of heaven upon our family. He said that *per-*

haps if there is a group of people who need the temple most in
their lives, it would be the young people and the parents of young
and growing families working out problems in the throes of life. It
would be parents of the youth and young adults who struggle to
live righteously in a world of tempting distractions.

Consider the promise to parents who are faithful to their
temple covenants:

"The Prophet Joseph Smith declared—and he never taught
more comforting doctrine—that the eternal sealings of faithful
parents and the divine promises made to them for valiant service
in the Cause of Truth, would save not only themselves but likewise their posterity. Though some of the sheep may wander, the
eye of the Shepherd is upon them, and sooner or later they will
feel the tentacles of Divine Providence reaching out after them
and drawing them back to the fold. Either in this life or the life
to come, they will return. They will have to pay their debt to jus-
tice; they will suffer for their sins; and may tread a thorny path,
but if it leads them at last, like the penitent prodigal, to a loving
and forgiving Father's heart and home, the painful experience
will not have been in vain. Pray for your careless and disobedient
children; hold on to them with your faith. Hope on, trust on, till
you see the salvation of God.

"Who are these straying sheep—these wayward sons and
daughters? They are children of the Covenant, heirs to the
promise, and have received, if baptized, the Gift of the Holy
Ghost, which makes manifest the things of God. Could all that
go for naught?" (Orson F. Whitney, in Conference Report, Apr.
1919, p. 118).

A longtime friend of mine has seen her eldest daughter
struggle, rebel, and draw far away from her family and the gospel.
Her second daughter has been faithful and obedient all of her life
and recently married in the temple. The weeks preceding the

wedding were hectic, overscheduled, and extremely stressful. My dear friend fully believed that the *most* she could do for this wayward daughter was to be faithful in attending the temple. Even during these busy weeks of wedding plans, she maintained her commitment to attend regularly. One week before the wedding, there was just no time to go—she simply had too many obligations. She was driving on the freeway, thinking about her being unable to go to the temple, when she was inspired that nothing else she had to do was as important as going that morning to the temple. She felt impressed that while it would be a sacrifice, sacrifice brings the blessings of heaven, and her wayward daughter needed these blessings. My friend felt she needed them too. She turned her car and drove straight to the temple.

The Lord gave Noah and his family an ark to raise them out of a filthy world, to protect them, to shelter, sustain, and preserve them through the flood and other dangers. He gave them an ark to ensure that they would continue on in this world and the world would continue on with them.

Our ark is the temple. It lifts us out of the filthy world. In the temple we find protection and shelter. We are sustained and preserved against the floods and dangers of Satan and the natural calamities of mortal life. We find the strength to carry on.

Our offerings have to be acceptable to the Lord. In ancient days, those offerings consisted of the best of the flock or field. Today, we often must sacrifice our time. President Washburn told me that the *casual* temple attender will not receive the blessings of the temple. Those who sacrifice will. What those sacrifices are is personal and individual. For someone who lives hours away from a temple, maybe once a month is a huge sacrifice. For someone who lives minutes away, maybe more of an offering is required. Each of us has a conscience and the right to be inspired as to what the Lord would have us do.

If we are born of the Spirit, we will be led to the temple. There we will be empowered with the Spirit, and the Spirit will teach us the truth—"things as they are, and . . . as they are to come"—through those truths, and by no other means will we overcome our weaknesses and overcome the world.

We go to sacrament meeting to renew our covenants of baptism; should we not come to the temple to renew our covenants of exaltation? True disciples of Christ want to be in the temple. This is part of what makes us great men and great women.

We do not rush into sacrament meeting, take the sacrament, and rush out. Similarly, we do not come to the temple to rush in, do a session, and rush out. It is important to take the proper time to worship, pray, and call down the blessings of heaven on our families.

A few months ago a lovely, faithful woman came to visit me. She had married a nonmember at a time in her life when she was less active. He is a good husband to her and a good father to their young family; he supports her in her Church activity. But she has never gone to the temple. Until recently she only thought about it casually. Lately, however, she has been filled with tender feelings and a desire to go. She is being led by the Holy Ghost, she has been born of the Spirit, and He is leading her to the temple. It will be a great blessing to her and her family.

I add my testimony to the power of the temple blessings in our lives. I have gone to the house of the Lord many times feeling weighed down by the cares of the world and the burdens of family life. In the temple I have found comfort and peace—almost immediately as I cross the threshold a quiet assurance envelops me.

My understanding has expanded and my memory has been enlarged. Sometimes I have had thoughts and ideas come into my mind in answer to my prayers right there while I was in the temple. But more often the answer comes after I leave the temple. The next day, or a few days later, or a week or two at the most, the answer or comfort does come—clearly, sometimes unexpectedly, but always as a clear witness that I have been heard and that the Lord remembers me.

President Ezra Taft Benson said: "In the peace of these lovely temples, sometimes we find solutions to the serious problems in life. Under the influence of the Spirit, sometimes pure knowledge flows to us there. Temples are places of personal revelation. When I have been weighed down by a problem or a difficulty, I have gone to the House of the Lord with a prayer in my heart for answers. These answers have come in clear and unmistakable ways" ("What I Hope You Will Teach Your Children about the Temple," *Ensign*, Aug. 1985, p. 8).

The Savior has invited us to learn of him. So we must ask ourselves: *How* do I learn of him? *Where* is he, literally and figuratively? The answers are "in the temple." This is why the Holy Ghost leads us to the temple if we are truly born of the Spirit. A temple-loving people will make the temple the centerpiece of their lives.

What are we working toward as individuals? To become more like Jesus Christ in thought, word, and deed. What are we working toward as a collective body of Latter-day Saints? To become a Zion people, a people led by Christ the King. There is a record of such a group of people who achieved that—the inhabitants of the city of Enoch. They overcame the world, literally. They were taken up. They overcame the world with the power of love for one another. I am persuaded that a temple-loving people will overcome the world with their power of love for one another.

Elder Vaughn J. Featherstone has taught: "Before the Savior comes the world will darken. There will come a period of time where even the elect will lose hope if they do not come to the temples. The world will be so filled with evil that the righteous will only feel secure within these walls. The Saints will come here not only to do vicarious work, but to find a haven of peace. They will long to bring their children here for safety's sake. . . . There will be greater hosts of unseen beings in the temple. Prophets of old as well as those in this dispensation will visit the temples. Those who attend will feel their strength and feel their companionship. We will not be alone in our temples.

"Our garments worn as instructed will clothe us in a manner as protective as temple walls. The covenants and ordinances will fill us with faith as a living fire. In a day of desolating sickness, scorched earth, barren wastes, sickening plagues, disease, destruction, and death, we as a people will rest in the shade of trees, we will drink from the cooling fountains. We will abide in places of refuge from the storm, we will mount up as on eagles' wings, we will be lifted out of an insane and evil world. We will be as fair as the sun and clear as the moon.

"The Savior will come and will honor His people. Those who are spared and prepared will be a temple-loving people. They will know Him. . . . Our children will bow down at His feet and worship Him as the Lord of Lords, the King of Kings. They will bathe His feet with their tears and He will weep, and bless them for having suffered through the greatest trials known to man. . . .

"Let us prepare them with faith to surmount every trial and every condition. We will do it in these holy, sacred temples" (address at the Manti Temple, April 1987).

In the temple we will be filled with the Holy Ghost; we will be able to return to the world "armed with power," with angels to attend us. We will be more able to always remember him so we may become more and more like him.

Always remembering him is a desire we nurture by our efforts to be valiant in our testimonies and to pass on a legacy of testimony.

To be valiant in our testimonies means we stand as witnesses of

God in all places and in all things and at all times (see Mosiah 18:9). Bearing our testimonies can sometimes test our faith. We will receive witnesses from what we read or from what another person says—important elements in the process of gaining a testimony. But it is quite another matter when the Holy Ghost confirms to us in our own hearts that what *we* have testified is true. To bear our testimonies and to stand as witnesses is a critical part of "remembering him."

"And now, I Moroni, . . . would show unto the world that faith is things which are hoped for and not seen; wherefore, dispute not because ye see not, for ye receive no witness until after the trial of your faith" (Ether 12:6).

A legacy of testimony requires a trial of faith. Something of great value is worth being cherished enough to pass on.

In the words of Elder Henry B. Eyring: "Some of the greatest opportunities to create and transmit a legacy of testimony cannot be planned. Tragedy, loss, and hurt often arrive unanticipated. How we react when we are surprised will tell our families whether what we have taught and testified lies deep in our hearts. Most of us will have taught our children of the power of the Savior to carry us through whatever befalls us. . . .

"When tragedy strikes or even when it looms, our families will have the opportunity to look into our hearts to see whether we know what we said we knew. Our children will watch, feel the Spirit confirm that we lived as we preached, remember that confirmation, and pass the story across the generations" (*To Draw Closer to God* [Salt Lake City: Deseret Book Co., 1997], p. 180).

There is a special promise recorded in the scriptures to those who will exercise such faith, even to those who fear their testimonies are weak. And if we will speak out with humility, real intent, and a desire to "always remember him," the promise will be fulfilled:

"Therefore, verily I say unto you, lift up your voices unto this people; speak the thoughts that I *shall* [note that it is in future tense] put into your hearts, and you shall not be confounded before men; for it *shall* [again note the future tense] be given you in the very hour, yea, in the very moment, what ye shall say. But a commandment I give unto you, that ye shall declare whatsoever thing ye declare in my name, in solemnity of heart, in the spirit of meekness, in all things. And I give unto you this promise, that inasmuch as ye do this the Holy Ghost shall be shed forth in bearing record unto all things whatsoever ye shall say" (D&C 100:5–8; emphasis added).

There may be those who would say that if you bear testimony when you doubt or don't really know or are struggling in deep difficulties or simply when your faith is weak that the testimony carries little or no meaning, that it is merely a series of commonly used LDS phrases.

Well, one thing is certain: those who say this will never know, because they will never exercise the faith needed to receive the witness after the trial of their faith. Testimony and the power of spiritual legacy will never come to the arrogant, the proud, the intellectual, the ones who fail to remember.

Elder Boyd K. Packer observed: "The Spirit and testimony of Christ will come to you for the most part *when*, and remain with you only *if*, you share it. In that process is the *very essence* of the gospel.

"Is not this a perfect demonstration of Christianity? You cannot find it, nor keep it, nor enlarge it unless and until you are willing to share it. It is by giving it away freely that it becomes yours" ("The Candle of the Lord," *Ensign*, Jan. 1983, p. 55).

So many great parents, good and noble men and women, have taught their children to love the Lord. By their examples of faith and enduring with hope through trials, great parents have testified to their children that they believe what they have taught. But even teaching and testifying has not seemed to benefit some children, and many great parents have seen part of their families reject this legacy.

I was visiting with some sisters when the conversation turned to a discussion about the promise made to parents who were faithful in temple covenants that their wayward children would return. The question was raised, even if our children return, what about the third and fourth generations and so on? One sister said, "That's where they *will be lost.*" I would like again to quote Elder Eyring:

"There is reason for us to have great hope and optimism. It comes first from our testimony of the nature of our Heavenly Father: he loves our family members. . . . It also comes from our testimony of the mission of Jesus Christ: he paid the price to redeem them. And it comes from our testimony of the restoration of priesthood keys. Because of that, the power is on the earth again to make convenants with God that seal families together, covenants which God honors.

"That is why we must not despair. As we offer the legacy of testimony to our families, some may not receive it. It may even seem to skip over generations. But God will reach out to offer the legacy again and again. More than we can imagine, our faithful effort to offer to our family the testimony we have of the truth will be multiplied in power and extended in time.

"We have all seen the evidence of that in families we have known. I saw it in South America as I looked into the faces of missionaries. Hundreds of them passed by me, shaking my hand and looking deeply into my eyes. I was nearly overwhelmed with the confirmation that these children of Father Lehi and of Sariah were there in the Lord's service because our Heavenly Father honors his promises to families. To nearly his last breath, Lehi taught and testified and tried to bless his children. Terrible tragedy came among his descendants when they rejected his testimony and the testimonies of other prophets and of the scriptures. But in the eyes and faces of those missionaries I felt confirmation that God has kept his promises to reach out to Lehi's covenant children—and that he will reach out to ours" (*To Draw Closer to God*, pp. 181–82).

We all make mistakes. We all have temptations. Great sorrows and disappointments come to each of us. This is a telestial world and we have telestial bodies. They get tired and sick and flabby.

We can't make ourselves sinless. We will live our mortal lives in this cycle of sinning and struggling to overcome sin. Then what hope do we have of becoming great men and great women, of becoming like Jesus Christ? How can we be assured of our place in the celestial kingdom when we can't even be sure tomorrow will be a sinless day for us?

In the Doctrine and Covenants is recorded a small description of those who will inherit the celestial kingdom. It is brief, but it is perhaps the most hopeful piece of doctrine taught to man. "These are they whose names are written in heaven, where God and Christ are the judge of all. These are they who are just men made perfect through Jesus the mediator of the new covenant, who wrought out this perfect atonement through the shedding of his own blood" (D&C 76:68–69).

It doesn't say "these are they who are perfect." It says clearly, "just men made perfect through Jesus." "Just" men and women are those who are filled with the desire to do right and to strive to do so even though their behavior doesn't always match that desire!

You and I cannot become perfect *without the Savior*. And that is the great hope we have and the great gift of the Atonement in our lives!

We continue to make our lives more difficult, more complicated, more full of risk if we try to struggle through life on our will alone. "For behold, it is as easy to give heed to the word of Christ, which will point to you a straight course to eternal bliss, as it was for our fathers to give heed to this compass, which would point unto them a straight course to the promised land. And now I say, is there not a type in this thing? For just as surely as this director did bring our fathers, by following its course, to the promised land, shall the words of Christ, if we follow their course, carry us beyond this vale of sorrow into a far better land of promise" (Alma 37:44–45).

True greatness lies in sacrifice, in denying ourselves. The inhabitants of the far better land of promise will be a generous people. They will have led mortal lives of small, quiet acts of service and love to their families and fellowmen. They will have given away their pride and denied themselves prejudice and selfishness. They will be a forgiving people. They will have submitted and yielded time and resources to help build the kingdom of God. They will have used their talents to uplift others, even serving missions in their aging years.

They will be loyal people—loyal to the Lord and to one another. They will have used their words to build others, not to judge or condemn. They will be of one heart and one mind with Jesus Christ. *They will be like him.*

The inhabitants of the "far better land of promise" will have had joy in this life in their common lot ordinary work of laundry, employment, menial tasks, groceries, car pools, childbearing, family life, and problems of every kind. They will have had fun in this mortal life and enjoyed, really enjoyed, the blessings of the Lord to his children. They will have heeded his words: "The good things which come of the earth, whether for food or raiment, or for houses, or for barns, or for orchards, or for gardens, or for vineyards; yea, all things which come of the earth, in the season thereof, are made for the benefit and the use of man, both to please the eye and to gladden the heart; yea, for food and for raiment, for taste and for smell, to strengthen the body and to enliven the soul. And it pleaseth God that he hath given all these things unto man" (D&C 59:17–20).

They will be temple-loving people, people who have been born of the Spirit, people who have sought the Spirit all their mortal lives. They didn't just wake up one morning and let the day fall in their lap. They sought the Spirit in their lives for direction and growth.

The inhabitants of the "far better land of promise" will be those who have lived lives such that their posterity knew those progenitors believed what they taught. They will have endured to the end.

These are the elements and the ingredients of great men and great women.

There may be some who would hear these words of truth that have been spoken and disregard them. These skeptics may think it all sounds too trite or perhaps not exciting enough.

One thing is certain: the skeptics will never know. The Holy Ghost will not tutor the proud, the arrogant, the intellectual, even the apathetic. He will come to those with humility and a "free heart."

King Hezekiah required the Levites to cleanse the temple after years of abandonment and misuse. Then he invited the people to come back to the house of the Lord and worship righteously. Many laughed him to scorn and mocked him. But many were humbled and "brought in sacrifices and thank offerings; and as many as were of a *free heart* burnt offerings" (2 Chronicles 29:31; emphasis added; see chapters 29–30).

My friend Michelle has lived in southern Nevada all of her

life. As the Church grew, many members of the wards she attended either moved to other wards or were in other wards because of boundary changes and divisions. Over the years her circle of acquaintances expanded and extended to all parts of the Las Vegas Valley.

After she married and began to raise a family, she and her husband moved several times in the Las Vegas area. She always went to church. In every ward she ever lived, there were always friends or family. She really knew she was expected to be at church.

One year, she and her husband and family moved to northern Nevada for a while. Suddenly she found herself in a new church experience. She knew no one in her ward. No family, no friends, no acquaintances, no one who really noticed if they were at church or not. She did not feel needed or included in the membership.

It was then that she realized she went to church not because others expected her to, or because she had a really responsible Church calling, or even that it was a great place to make new friends. She realized that she went because she wanted to go. Her heart was willing and devoted to the Savior. He knew she was there. She was there because she wanted to partake of the sacrament and was willing to "always remember him."

The Savior has invited us to greatness. He has invited us to become like him, and he has shown us our path of duty. He asks us to have a "free heart," a willing and devoted heart.

The Savior spoke very little during the nine hours he hung on the cross. Only seven sentences are recorded. One of those was to make sure his mother would be safe, protected, and comforted. Another sustained and encouraged one of the thieves who hung with him. But the most amazing sentence spoke of forgiveness to those who had crucified him. He was generous to his last breath, even in his agony.

He never had any luxuries—his work was what the world today calls blue-collar, that of a carpenter. There are no contemporary remarks recorded of his stature or his physical appearance. He was not known then or now for any contribution to the arts or sciences. And yet millions are accepting the invitation to be like him.

And as the host who has issued the invitation, he isn't just standing at the gate waiting for us to arrive. He is giving us the directions home. He is actually assisting us in finding our way, our path. What a comfort to each of us that we can hear him, even see the road home down a path of duty, if we will "always remember him."

The invitation is to become like him. If our "memory" serves us well, we will become great men and great women and he will abide with us forever.

INDEX

Accountability, 24
Adam and Eve, 41
Addiction, 24
Adoption, 99–100
Adversity, 71–72
Agency, 20, 22, 24, 25, 27, 34–35,
    49, 74
Airport (story), 13, 14, 70–71
Alice in Wonderland, 42
Angels, 32, 41
Anger, 20, 96
Animals, 74, 77
Ashton, Marvin J., missionary story
    of, 62–63
Atheists, 33
Atonement. *See* Jesus Christ, atone-
    ment of
Attitude, 20

Baptism, 21, 75
Battle swords, 49–72
Battle words, 48–49
Beggar (story), 81
Benjamin (son of Jacob), 28, 29
Benson, Ezra Taft, on changing
    human nature, 40–41
  on duty of every young man, 16, 17
  on temples, 108
Blaming, 24, 38–39
Blueberries (story), 89–90
Body (analogy), 77, 79
Book of Mormon, 17, 71
Boys Chorus of Southern Nevada, 32
Brigham Young University, 13,
    22–23, 50

Brotherhood, 83
Brown, Hugh B., on judgment, 72

California, 53–54
Callings, 6, 24, 79, 85
Calvary, 68
Canada, 11–12
Canfield, Steve, 53–54
Capernaum, 80
Carnegie, Dale, on lemons, 30
Celestial kingdom, 62, 113
Cerebral palsy, 30–34
Chance, 2
Charity, 79, 80–86
Children, 56
  wayward, 105–6, 111–13
Choices. *See* Agency
Christianity, 69–70
Churchill, Winston, 46
Clark, Brother, 86–87
Commandments, 4, 6, 7, 11, 15, 21,
    24, 43, 63, 66, 67, 75
Commitment, 3, 4, 23, 60, 101, 103
Confidence, 27, 34
Consistency, 24
Contention, 25
Conversations, 78–80
Conversion, 91
Corinthians, 77, 79
Courage, 30, 45, 46, 47, 52, 68, 69,
    70
Covenants, 4, 107
Criticism, 79–80, 101

Darkness, 49, 50

Deacons (story), 81–86
Dentist (story), 53–54
Depression, 50
Designer (story), 37–38
Despair, 102
Determination, 60
Diabetes (story), 50–52
Disappointment, 58, 113
Discipleship, 55
Discouragement, 102
Disneyland (story), 81–86
Donne, John, on memory, 102
Duty, a path of, 1–18, 24, 59, 73–74,
     96

Eastern Germany, 64–65
Eden, 19, 41
Education Week, 13
Egypt, 28–29
Endurance, 3, 7, 49, 52, 111
Ephesus, 69
Esther, 73–74, 94
Eve, 41
Exaltation, 107
Example, in charity, 80–86
     in faith, 87–90
     of parents, 111–12
     in purity, 90–94
     in spirit, 86–87
     in word and conversation, 78–80
Excuses, 24, 38–39
Eyring, Henry B., on his father, 8–10
     on legacy of testimony, 110, 112
Eyring, Henry (father of Henry B.),
     8–10

Faith, 2–3, 21, 25, 48, 59–60, 111
     example in, 87–90
Fame, 1–2
Family home evening, 91
Family Home Evening (video), 16
Farm property (story), 11–12
Fasting, 93

Fault-finding, 24, 38–39
Fear, 20, 34, 41, 48, 50, 73
Featherstone, Vaughn J., on temples,
     108–9
Forgiveness, 29, 62, 97, 101
Foundations, 21
Free agency. *See* Agency
Freedom, 35, 41, 48
Friendship, 82–83, 86

Garden of Eden, 19, 41
Generosity, 96–101
Germany, 64–65
Gethsemane, 50, 68, 97
Goshen, 29
Gossip, 79
Grant, Heber J., on the path of duty,
     4, 6
Gratitude, 17, 100
Greatness, Holy Ghost inspires us
     to, 102
     ingredients of, 115
     Jesus invites us to, 116
     of Joseph, 26, 27
     of our lives, 94
     of Paul, 49
     quest for, 19, 20–21, 22, 23,
         41–42, 100
     of Spencer W. Kimball, 45
     true, 1–18
Guilt, 20, 36, 41

Haight, David B., on command-
     ments, 15
Handicapped boy (story), 30–34,
     60–62
Hanks, Marion D., on withholding
     love, 98
Happiness, 10, 19–20, 36
Hawaii, 86–87
Hezekiah, 115
Hinckley, Gordon B., on pioneers,
     58

testimony of, 71
Holy Ghost, born of the, 115
    as a comforter, 51
    companionship of the, 41
    and freedom, 35, 40
    gift of the, 101
    and hope, 6
    and humility, 115
    inspires us to greatness, 102
    and meekness, 7, 21, 34, 43
    and missionary preparation, 17
    seeking the, 101
    and temples, 109
    and testimony, 109–10
    will lead us to temple, 103, 106,
        107, 108
Home teaching, 2–3, 87
Hope, 6–7, 22, 49, 50, 68
House (analogy), 55–56
Humility, 3, 7, 55, 96, 98, 115

Independence, 34–35
Integrity, 24
Iron Curtain, 64

Jacob (Bible patriarch), 25, 29
Jesus Christ, atonement of, 48, 64,
        101
    as the greatest of us all, 97
    becoming like, 108
    Capernaum sermon of, 42
    greatness of, 50
    invites us to greatness, 116
    is a friend, 86
    on love, 75
    murmuring disciples of, 80
    one heart with, 3–4
    and perfection, 113
    and repentance, 40
    second coming of, 60, 79
    "the heart and a willing mind," 22
    walked on water, 55
    "why has thou forsaken me," 46

Jim (story), 81–86
Joseph (son of Jacob), 25–30
Joy, 10, 48
Judgment, 72, 78–79, 114

Kimball, Spencer W., greatness of,
        45–46
    on perspective, 52–53
    on suffering, 64
Kindness, 80
Kirtland Temple, 104–5
Laman, 26, 57
Lamanites, 66
Las Vegas, Nev., 116
Las Vegas Temple, 60, 103
Latter-day Saint life, 8, 96
Laws, 36
Leaders, criticism of, 79
Leah, 25
Legacy, 87–88, 110, 112
Lehi, 6
Lemons (story), 30
Lemuel, 26, 57
Levites, 115
Lewis, C. S., living house analogy of,
        55–56
Linda (story), 90–92
Living house (analogy), 55–56
Loneliness, 46
Los Angeles, Calif., 37–38
Love, 2, 12, 21, 25, 29, 43, 75–76,
        79, 83, 84, 99–101
    withholding, 98
Loyalty, 3, 114
Luck, 2

MacDonald, George, living house
        analogy of, 55–56
Maxwell, Neal A., on good cheer,
        57–58
    on keeping the commandments, 4
    on meekness, 39
    on memory, 102

on patience, 64–66
on perspective, 54–55, 59
on pressing forward, 49–50
on purposes of life, 54
Meekness, 7, 21, 34, 39, 43, 96, 97
Memory, 102, 117
Michelle (story), 115–16
Misery, 20
Missionaries, 12, 13–14, 15–17,
    60–62, 62–63, 86–87, 91–92
Missionary Training Center, 13, 14, 17
Mormon Battalion, 14
Mothers, 13–14
Motivation, 1
Murmuring, 57, 80
Music, 32, 100
Muslims, 69–70

National Medal of Science, 10
Natural man, 24, 41, 102
Nauvoo, Ill., 14
Nazis, 46
Nephi, 57
    on pressing forward, 50
Nephites, 66
Nevada, 60, 103, 115–16
Noah, 10, 106
North Carolina, 50–51

Obedience, and duty, 6, 7
    and greatness, 23, 24, 26
    and the Holy Ghost, 22
    and independence, 34
    of Joseph of Egypt, 29
    and love, 76
    and meekness, 21, 39–40, 43
    of missionary, 63
    and protection, 55
    and purpose, 62
    and self-mastery, 36
Okazaki, Chieko, "God wants you," 22
Onion patch (story), 9–10
Oregon, 90

Packer, Boyd K., on sharing testi-
    mony, 111
Parents, 111
Patience, 3, 64–66, 79, 98
Paul, as a battle sword, 68–72
    body analogy of, 77, 79
    on example, 92
    greatness of, 49
    on judgment, 72
    on pressing forward, 49–50
Peace, 12, 36, 48, 52, 61, 99–100
Perfection, 5, 6, 22, 43, 113
Performance, 74–75
Perspective, 52–62
Peter, 42, 59
    walked on water, 55
Pharaoh, 28
Pioneers, 58
Pioneer (story), 14–15
Plan of salvation, 55
Pollyanna mentality, 57
Potiphar, 26, 27
Praise, 100–101
Prayer, 16, 31–32, 42, 46, 52, 56,
    66–68, 90, 92–93
Prejudice, 114
Premortality, 19
Press (battle sword), 49–52
Pride, 27, 56, 98
Prizes, 1
Prophets, 18
Provo, Utah, 13, 17
Purity, 90–94
Purpose, 62–64

Rachel, 25
Rachel (story), 92–94
Rector, Hartman Jr., on Joseph,
    29–30
Repentance, 24, 40, 42, 55, 62, 101
Resurrection, 8
Revelation, 67, 103, 108
Road rage, 96

Robinson, Stephen E., on desire and performance, 74–75
on staying in the kingdom, 62
Rodriguez, Brother, 88–89
Rose, Anne Marie, 58–59
R-rated movies, 42
Rules, 36

Sabbath day, 42
Sacrament, 4, 88, 89, 107
Sacrifice, 18, 70, 81, 93, 97–98, 106
Salt Lake City, Utah, 13, 14
San Francisco, Calif., 53
Satan, 10, 40, 46–47, 47, 66, 98, 102, 104, 106
Scientists, 34
Scriptures, 42, 49
Second Coming, 60, 79
Self-control, 39
Self-denial, 97
Self-doubt, 20, 45
Self-esteem, 20, 22, 25, 29, 39–40, 42, 76
Selfishness, 98, 114
Self-mastery, 36, 39
Selma (story), 50–52
Service, 2, 80, 99, 101
Singing, 32, 100
Sins, 6, 7, 21
Smith, Emma, 57
Smith, Hans, 30–34, 66
Smith, Joseph, Jr., "no unhallowed hand," 76
testimony of, 17
on victory, 72
on wayward children, 105
Smith, Joseph F., on true greatness, 2
Spirit, example in, 86–87
Stephen, 69
Submission, 63, 67

Suffering, 64
Swenson, Sharon Lee, on giving oneself, 22–23

Tails, 49
Telestial world, 2, 113
Temples, 60–61, 68, 103–9, 114, 115
Temptation, 41
Temptations, 112–13
Testimony, 5, 71, 100, 109–12
Thoughts, 49
Timothy, 92
Tithing, 89–90, 96
Trials, 2, 14, 47, 50, 52, 67, 111
Tribulations. See Trials
Trust, 3, 55, 56

Vagrant (story), 81
Victory, 45–72, 74
Visiting teachers, 2–3
Volleyball (story), 58–59

War in Heaven, 46–47
Washburn, J. Ballard, on temples, 103, 104, 106–7
Washington, D.C., 10
Wayward children, 105–6, 111-12
Weakness, 40, 79
Wedding (story), 105–6
Weight loss (story), 35–36
White House, 10
Whitney, Orson F., on wayward children, 105
Winepress, 50
Words, 78–80
Work, 2, 3
World War II, 48

Young, Brigham, on obedience, 10